OFF~STAGE!

Sketches from the English Teaching Theatre

Teachers' Book

Doug Case and Ken Wilson

Photographs by Richard Gibb

H·E·B

HEINEMANN EDUCATIONAL BOOKS
LONDON

Heinemann Educational Books Ltd
22 Bedford Square, London WC1B 3HH
LONDON EDINBURGH MELBOURNE AUCKLAND
HONG KONG SINGAPORE KUALA LUMPUR NEW DELHI
IBADAN NAIROBI JOHANNESBURG
EXETER (NH) KINGSTON PORT OF SPAIN

ISBN 0 435 28033 3
(Students' Book ISBN 0 435 28032 5)
(Tapes ISBN 0 435 28034 1)
(Cassettes ISBN 0 435 28035 X)

First Published 1979
Reprinted 1981 (twice), 1984

Text set in 10/11½ pt VIP Sabon and 10/11 pt VIP Helvetica.
Printed and bound in Great Britain by Butler & Tanner Ltd, Frome and London

ACKNOWLEDGEMENTS

We would like to thank BBC English by Radio and Television for permission to reproduce the 'Ticket Inspector' sketch, which was originally written by Doug Case for the radio series 'Let's Speak English', and then adapted for the ETT's stage show. Information in the Customs Notice Number 1 (*The Customs Officer*) is reproduced with the permission of the Controller of Her Majesty's Stationery Office. This information is only correct at the time of printing and is subject to alteration. The extract from the Highway Code (*Gerry Brown's Driving Test*) is also with the permission of HMSO.

For information about the activities of the ETT, please write to: The English Teaching Theatre, 40 Shaftesbury Avenue, London W1V 8HJ

We would also like to express our thanks to these people:
– to John Haycraft, for having the original idea for the ETT, and for constant support and encouragement ever since;
– to Jeremy Harrison and Piers Plowright, who first gave the show a style and identity;
– to all the members of the ETT, past and present, particularly to those who performed the sketches in this book with us during the 1974–78 tours: John Colclough, Susanne Elliott, Lawrence Fitzgerald, Kieran Fogarty, Bernard Fox, Roy Garner, Judy Garton-Sprenger, Sheila Hanley, Hazel Imbert, David Lochner, Magee, Coralyn Sheldon, Russ Shipton, Terry Tomscha and Hugh Trethowan;
– to all the organizations who have helped us with our tours, particularly International House, the British Council, BBC English by Radio and Television, the British Tourist Authority, British Airways, Air France and the Flemish Association of Teachers of EFL;
– and most of all, to all the teachers and students who have been our audiences, organizers and hosts, for their help, kindness, hospitality and enthusiasm.

Doug Case, Ken Wilson, July 1978

Contents

E = Elementary; I = Intermediate; A = Advanced (see Introduction, p. 7)

S & U = The main structural points practised in the sketch.

A & F = The attitudes and functions practised in the Communicating exercises. Other points are practised in other sections of each unit but are not itemized here. (See Introductory page to each unit.)

Introduction

The English Teaching Theatre

The ETT is a unique kind of theatre. It began in 1969 at International House, London, when the director, John Haycraft, said to one of his teachers, Jeremy Harrison: 'Why don't we have a theatre specially for students of English?'.

Starting with summer seasons in London, we have gradually expanded our activities, and since 1974 the ETT has been a permanent theatre-group, performing in schools, teacher-training colleges, universities and theatres all over the world. Countries visited include Belgium, Denmark, France, Germany, Greece, Holland, Italy, Mexico, Norway, Portugal, Spain, Sweden, Switzerland, Turkey and Yugoslavia. Every year, more than 250 performances are given, and the show is seen on stage by more than 75,000 people – and on TV by many more.

The shows are revues consisting of sketches and songs and involving a lot of audience participation, and the format evolved from a style of teaching in which the use of sketches, songs and role-playing is considered very useful.

'Perhaps the most interesting aspect of the English Teaching Theatre is that it involves the audience and makes students aware that English is not just words, structures and idioms but that it is a lively, dramatic and versatile means of communication. From another point of view, it is valuable in showing the language teacher dramatic techniques which he can use in the classroom. It emphasises, too, that learning and teaching can and should be pleasurable.' John Haycraft – International House

The Book

There are fifteen sketches in the book, and all are recorded on the accompanying cassette or tape.

Each gives practice with specific language-points, both structural and functional.

The scripts are accompanied by role-playing and improvisation activities, as well as exercises for listening and reading comprehension, writing and discussion topics, and puzzles.

Each unit is based on one sketch and the Students' Book contains the following sections within a unit:

- The text of the sketch, with photographs
- Questions for Listening Comprehension
- A Reading Comprehension exercise
- Word Puzzle
- Communicating
- In Your Own Words
- Writing
- What do you think?

In the Teachers' Book, each unit contains all the material in the Students' Book. Notes for the teacher are added to each exercise, and there are also the following extra sections:

- An Introductory page
- Further Role-playing Activities
- Pronunciation Practice

The Contents of a Unit and Suggestions For Use

The symbol * indicates sections which only appear in the Teachers' Book.

For all the sections which appear in the Students' Book, the Teachers' Book gives specific suggestions for use in the Notes inserted in the appropriate places. Some general suggestions are given here, however.

1 Introductory Page *

This page contains:

- a brief introduction to the sketch.
- ATTITUDES AND FUNCTIONS. A list, with examples, of the main attitudes and functions which occur in the sketch, and which are practised in the 'Communicating' section and in the Role-playing activities.

- STRUCTURE AND USAGE. A list, with examples, of the main structural points in the sketch.
- NOTE THE FOLLOWING WORDS AND EXPRESSIONS. Words and phrases which may prove difficult for the students. These are listed here for reference, as you may feel it necessary to present and practise some of them before the students listen to the sketch. It is not advisable to present them *all* beforehand, however, as the students should be encouraged to deduce meanings where possible from their listening. Where a particular word or expression should definitely *not* be presented beforehand (because this would spoil the surprise of a joke, for example), this is indicated.
- SUGGESTED PRELIMINARY PRACTICE. Ideas for an activity to introduce the sketch, based on either the main structural point or one of the attitudes and functions. These are usually short oral activities, involving mime, questions and answers, simple blackboard pictures and so on. It is also possible to do the exercises from the 'Communicating' section before listening to the sketch in many cases.
- PRELIMINARY QUESTIONS. Three questions to give the students before they listen to the sketch. These can be read to the students or written on the blackboard, and are designed to give a definite purpose to the listening. The first listening to the sketch will be mainly for enjoyment, but at the same time the students will be listening in order to extract a few important pieces of information. After the first listening to the sketch, the answers to these Preliminary Questions should be discussed. (Note that the three Preliminary Questions for the first sketch, 'The Ticket Inspector' are the type of questions which can be used before *any* sketch.)

2 Text of the Sketch

As recorded on the cassette or tape. The text is divided into four or five short sections and the Listening Comprehension Questions and re-enacting ('In Your Own Words') are based on these divisions.

The text is essentially for reference: for silent reading after the oral work on the sketch, for 'look and listen' (following while listening to the recording after the oral work), or for consulting when necessary as part of the other activities (in solving the Word Puzzle, for example).

In these texts, a dash (–) is used at the end of a line when a speaker is interrupted, and 3 dots (. . .) when a speaker hesitates.

3 Listening Comprehension ('Questions' in the Students' Book)

Questions to be used after the students have listened to the sketch. After the first listening to the sketch and the follow-up discussion of the Preliminary Questions, the students can listen to the sketch again, answering the questions after each section. Any words and expressions which are unfamiliar can be discussed and practised here. The questions could be written on the blackboard instead of having the students refer to their books. They can be answered with the class as a whole, or the students can decide on their answers in groups first. You may of course like to invent more questions of your own, or ask the students to invent their own extra questions.

4 Reading Comprehension (Specific heading in each unit in the Students' Book: 'Read and explain', 'True or False?', 'Read and Complete', etc.)

There is a variety of reading material in this section, including letters (Unit 8), instructions (Unit 3), anecdotes (Unit 2) and newspaper advertisements (Unit 4), each relating to the theme of the sketch. The section encourages careful silent reading with a purpose – to extract information, to correct mistakes, and so on. The activities are all suitable for the students to do individually, in pairs or in groups, and the Teachers' Notes give specific suggestions on how this can be done.

5 Word Puzzle

These puzzles can be solved by referring to the language used in the sketch. If desired, a competitive element can be introduced by making the solving into a team game.

6 *Communicating*

Short activities designed to practise individual attitudes and functions demonstrated in the sketch – practical everyday uses of language such as apologizing, making suggestions, complimenting or showing disbelief. Appropriate language (points from the sketch and related language) is presented in the form of tables or short dialogues. These are accompanied by notes explaining whether the expressions are formal or colloquial.

These activities are generally designed for oral practice in twos or threes. After listening to the teacher giving the first example as a model, the students should practise in their pairs or groups, while the teacher monitors them and helps as necessary. As there are normally two exercises, some groups could begin with the first and some with the second, and then switch over.

7 *In Your Own Words*

The key words from each section of the sketch are listed here. These serve as a guide when the students re-enact the sketch in their own words.

The students should work in groups, using the prompt-words to guide them – either from the book or written on the blackboard or on small slips of paper or card. They should follow the general development of the sketch, but feel free to express it in their own words and add their own ideas. Go round and help the groups as they do this. (Where necessary, male characters from the taped version of the sketch can be played by female students, and vice-versa.)

The students can re-enact the whole sketch in their groups, and then 'perform' their version for the rest of the class if they wish. (Such 'performances' can be very enjoyable, but should not be considered essential, as the most valuable practice takes place in the groups.) Alternatively, each group can prepare a different section of the sketch, and these sections can then be combined into a continuous re-enacting. This can result in lively 'performances', especially if the groups build on any new ideas which the other groups have introduced.

In the Teachers' Notes to this section, suggestions are made for 'props'. For re-enacting in the classroom, these are always simple and easily obtainable objects.

8 *Further Role-playing Activities**

Situations for role-playing in which the students can make imaginative use of the language developed in the unit. The important aspect of these activities is the spontaneous use of language. Often prompts are given for situations similar to the original sketch (e.g. Unit 1), or the idea of the sketch is developed along different lines (e.g. Unit 4). Specific instructions for organizing each activity are given.

In contrast to the 'Communicating' exercises, each of which focusses on a particular communicative skill (see above), the activities suggested here provide speaking practice in a wider context.

9 *Pronunciation Practice**

Exercises on interesting features of stress and intonation which have occurred in the sketch. These exercises are usually based on short sections of the recorded sketch, and take one of two forms: careful *listening* to the tape for recognition of moods and attitudes conveyed by the stress and intonation, or *oral practice* with particular patterns of stress and intonation.

10 *Writing*

This section provides writing exercises of several types, including letters (Units 6, 7), dialogues (Unit 4), newspaper articles (Units 9, 11) and form-filling (Unit 5).

Oral preparation in class is always useful with writing activities, and students should also be encouraged to make notes before attempting their final version. This can be done individually, in pairs or in groups. The final versions can then be written in class or at home.

11 *What Do You Think?*

Topics based on themes from the sketch, designed to promote classroom discussion. It is not always easy to conduct discussions with a large group of students, and it is helpful if

the class can be divided initially into several small groups. Each group can then be given the chance to discuss the topic, or one aspect of it. After this, the groups can express their opinions to the class as a whole. Points which are raised can be summarized on the blackboard.
It is useful if the students are familiar with some of the phrases used in conducting discussions. For example:

To state an opinion
'I think . . . .'
'In my opinion . . . .'
'I've always thought that . . . .'
'If you ask me . . . .'
To ask for an opinion
'What do you think?'
'What do you think of . . . .?'
'Do you think that . . . .?'
'I think . . . ., don't you?'
'Do you agree?'
To clarify a point
'No, I didn't mean that . . . . What I meant was . . . .'
'When I say ". . . . .", I mean . . . .'
'When you say ". . . . .", do you mean . . . .?'

To agree with someone
'I agree.'
'I agree with you (about that).'
'Yes, that's right.'
'That's true.'
To disagree with someone
'I disagree.'
'I don't agree.'
'I'm not sure I agree with you.'
'You have a point, but (don't you think that) . . . .'
'You're not serious, are you?'/'You must be joking.' (*familiar*)
To interrupt someone
'Sorry to interrupt, but . . . .'
'Just a minute . . . .'/'Hold on . . . .' (*familiar*)

If a few of these phrases are taught beforehand, the discussions will run more smoothly.

Selecting Material
It is important to remember that the book is not a course. It aims to provide enjoyable material to be used *alongside* the course your students are following. Therefore, it is not necessary to work through the book from beginning to end.
You could select a sketch according to its subject matter, according to the main structural points it practises, or according to the main functional points it practises.
As can be seen from the structures and functions included (listed in the alphabetical index at the back of this book), the sketches are most suitable for early intermediate students, but they can be used at a variety of levels.
On the introductory page to each unit, the level at which the sketch is most suitable is indicated (Elementary, Intermediate or more Advanced). Exercises within each unit which are more demanding than the level indicated are marked: * in the Teachers' Book. (If desired, exercises marked in this way – mostly Role-playing and Discussion activities – can also be used at a lower level with careful preparation and control.)
Just as it is not necessary to work through the book from beginning to end, it is also not necessary to work through a complete unit from beginning to end if you do not wish to. The various exercises based on each sketch provide material for several lessons.
We hope that you and your students enjoy using the material in 'Off-stage!' – and that we may have the opportunity of seeing you 'on stage' with the ETT one day.

Doug Case
Ken Wilson
July 1978

1
The Ticket Inspector

This sketch was first performed in July 1975. It was originally written for the BBC English by Radio series 'Let's Speak English', and then adapted for the ETT's stage-show. The script here is exactly as used in the stage-show, with one small exception: In the stage-show, the names which the passenger uses (at the end of section III) were varied to suit current affairs (e.g. Henry Kissinger, Leonid Brezhnev) and local personalities (e.g. the Prime Minister of the country where the performance was taking place, a locally known pop singer, etc.).
The sketch is suitable for Elementary students and above.

Attitudes and Functions
Refusing Offers
No, thanks.

Giving Personal Details
What is your name, sir?
– Mickey Mouse. M-O-U-S-E.

Explaining Clearly
I'm not *selling* tickets, sir.
No, sir. I mean: This is a *first-class* compartment.
Sir, I am a ticket inspector. I inspect tickets.
Not *now*, sir. At the next station.

Giving Instructions
Please leave the train.

Surprise
Mine? Me, sir? O.K.?

Structure and Usage
Main Point
Present Simple and Present Continuous tenses
e.g. I'm not selling tickets, sir.
I never buy a ticket.
You're travelling on a train. When people travel on a train, they always buy a ticket.

Other Points
Possessive Adjectives and Pronouns
e.g. Mine?
– Yes, yours. Your ticket.
'going to' with Infinitive
e.g. What are you going to do?
– I'm going to write your name in my book.

Note the Following Words and Expressions
compartment steward It's in the book, sir. I see.

Suggested Preliminary Practice
Use mimes to practise the Present Simple tense, in its use to express habitual actions. Mime various professions and ask the students to guess the professions from the mimes. The sequence for each one could be:
Teacher: (*Mime of cleaning a window*) What am I? What's my job?
Students: (You're) a window-cleaner.
Teacher: What do window-cleaners do?
Students: They clean windows.
Other examples could be: bus-driver/street-sweeper/songwriter. Then use other professions where the second answer is less obvious: e.g. footballer/artist/waiter.
Then allow the students to mime some professions for the rest of the class to guess and comment on in the same way.

Preliminary Questions
1 How many speakers were there?
2 Who were they?
3 How did they feel at the end?

1

The Ticket Inspector

SCENE — A compartment on a train

CHARACTERS — A passenger on a train
A ticket inspector
A steward and a waiter

I

The passenger is sitting in a compartment on a train. He is reading a newspaper. The steward opens the door.

STEWARD Coffee!

PASSENGER No, thanks.

The passenger closes the door, and continues reading. The waiter opens the door.

WAITER Seats for dinner!

PASSENGER No, thanks.

The passenger closes the door again, and continues reading. The ticket inspector opens the door.

INSPECTOR Tickets!

PASSENGER No, thanks.

INSPECTOR Pardon?

PASSENGER I don't want a ticket, thank you.

INSPECTOR I'm not *selling* tickets, sir.

PASSENGER No?

INSPECTOR No. I want to *see your* ticket.

PASSENGER Oh, I haven't got a ticket.

INSPECTOR You haven't got a ticket?

PASSENGER No. I never buy a ticket.

INSPECTOR Why not?

PASSENGER Well, they *are very* expensive, you know.

INSPECTOR Sir, you're travelling on a train. When people travel on a train, they always buy a ticket.

PASSENGER Er –

INSPECTOR And *this* is a first-class compartment.

PASSENGER Yes, it *is* very nice, isn't it?

INSPECTOR No, sir. I mean: This is a *first-class* compartment. When people travel in a first-class compartment, they always buy a first-class ticket.

II *They look at each other for a moment.*

PASSENGER No, they don't.

INSPECTOR What?

PASSENGER A lot of people don't buy tickets. The Queen doesn't buy a ticket, does she? Eh? Eh?

INSPECTOR No, sir, but *she's* a famous person.

PASSENGER And what about you? Where's yours?

INSPECTOR Mine?

PASSENGER Yes, yours. Your ticket. Have *you* got a ticket?

INSPECTOR Me, sir?

PASSENGER Yes, you.

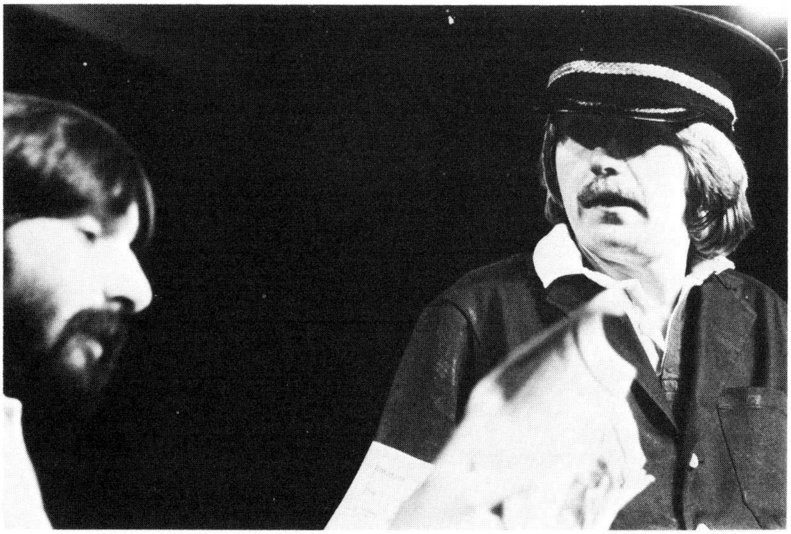

	INSPECTOR	No, I haven't got a ticket.
	PASSENGER	Ooh – are you a famous person?
	INSPECTOR	(*Flattered:*) Famous? Well, not very – (*Back to normal:*) Sir, *I* am a ticket inspector. I inspect tickets. Are you going to show me your ticket?
	PASSENGER	No, I haven't got a ticket.
	INSPECTOR	I see.
III		*The ticket inspector puts his hand into his pocket.*
	PASSENGER	What are you going to do?
	INSPECTOR	I'm going to write your name in my book.
	PASSENGER	Oh.
	INSPECTOR	What is your name, sir?
	PASSENGER	Mickey Mouse.
		The inspector begins to write.
	INSPECTOR	Mickey –
	PASSENGER	– Mouse. M-O-U-S-E.
		The inspector stops writing.
	INSPECTOR	Your *name*, sir?
	PASSENGER	Karl Marx? William Shakespeare? Charles Dickens?
IV	INSPECTOR	I see, sir. Well, if you're not going to tell me your name, please leave the train.
	PASSENGER	Pardon?
	INSPECTOR	Leave the train.
	PASSENGER	I can't.
	INSPECTOR	You can't what?
	PASSENGER	I can't leave the train.
	INSPECTOR	Why not?
	PASSENGER	It's moving.
	INSPECTOR	Not *now*, sir. At the next station.
	PASSENGER	Oh.
	INSPECTOR	It's in the book, sir. When you travel by train, you buy a ticket, and if you don't buy a ticket, you –
	PASSENGER INSPECTOR	– leave the train.
	INSPECTOR	Here we are, sir. We're coming to a station. Please leave the train now.
	PASSENGER	Now?
	INSPECTOR	Yes, sir. I'm sorry, but –
	PASSENGER	Oh, that's O.K.
	INSPECTOR	– it's in the book, and – What did you say?
	PASSENGER	I said: 'That's O.K.'
	INSPECTOR	O.K.?
	PASSENGER	Yes, this is my station. Goodbye.
		The passenger leaves the train.

Listening Comprehension

Questions

I 1 Did the passenger want coffee?
2 Did he have a ticket?
3 Was it a first or second-class compartment?

II 4 Why did the passenger mention the Queen?
5 Why did the ticket inspector say 'Mine'?

III 6 What was the passenger's name?
7 Why did the ticket inspector want to write down the passenger's name?

IV 8 Did the passenger buy a ticket?
9 Why did he leave the train?
10 Who was happier at the end?

Even though most of these questions are straightforward factual questions, and some of them could be answered with a simple 'Yes' or 'No', encourage the students to add remarks amplifying their answers: for example, Q.1. 'No. He said "No, thanks" to the steward.'; Q.2. 'No. He said he never bought a ticket, because they were very expensive.' Questions 4 and 5 should make the students refer to the attitudes of the speakers: the passenger's wanting to change the subject, and the ticket inspector's surprise.

Reading Comprehension

True or False?

Read this text about the sketch. Say which of the sentences are *true* and which are *false*. If a sentence is false, say why.

> The passenger was watching the countryside through the train window, when the steward came into the compartment. He had some coffee, but did not go to the dining-car for dinner. He was travelling in a first-class compartment, but he did not have a first-class ticket. He only had a second-class ticket. He told the ticket inspector that he was a famous person, and so he never bought a ticket. The ticket inspector wrote his name in his book, and told him to leave the train. At the next station, the passenger got off the train, very angry.

Allow the students to read the text silently on their own, or in groups with one student reading it aloud to the others. After reading it, they should note down whether the sentences are true or false. Notice that most of the sentences are true only in part, so the students should look very carefully at the details. Then discuss which sentences are false, and why. Encourage the students to refer back to the sketch: 'This sentence is false because . . .'

Word Puzzle

When all the vertical columns are filled, the letters in the box will spell a word – a part of a train. All the words are in the sketch on pp. 9–11.

1 When you travel on a train, you must buy a . . . .
2 The ticket inspector wanted to write the man's name in his . . . .
3 The man said his surname was . . . .
4 Someone who inspects tickets is a ticket . . . .
5 When the . . . . came into the compartment, the man said he didn't want any coffee.
6 The man was sitting in a . . . . compartment.
7 The . . . . told the man about the seats for dinner.

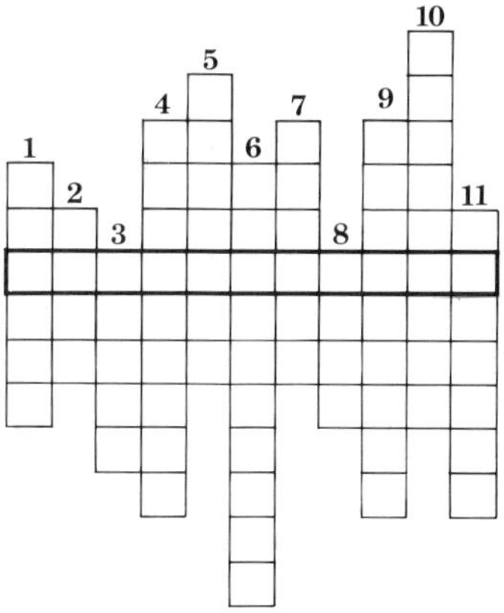

8 The second surname the man gave was . . . .
9 The man didn't buy a ticket, because they were very . . . .
10 The . . . . left the train very happily.
11 He was happy because he got off at his . . . .

Solution: 1 ticket 2 book 3 Mouse 4 inspector 5 steward 6 first-class 7 waiter 8 Marx 9 expensive 10 passenger 11 station. This produces the word 'compartment' in the box.

Communicating

1 Accepting and Refusing Offers

In the sketch, the passenger refused coffee and dinner, saying 'No, thanks'. In pairs, practise accepting and refusing offers. Use expressions from this table:

A:	Coffee? Tea? Do you want some beer? Would you like some cider?	B:	Yes, please. Yes, please. I'd love some. ----------------------------------- No, thanks./No, thank you. Not just now, thanks.

2 Giving Personal Details (Spelling)

Look at these lines from the sketch:

Ticket inspector	: What is your name, sir?
Passenger	: Mickey Mouse.
Ticket inspector	: Mickey –
Passenger	: – Mouse. M-O-U-S-E.

Practise in pairs. One person is a ticket inspector, policeman or other official, asking for the other person's name and address. The other person should give a name and address (real or invented) and spell it. The official should write it down.

Exercise 1: After practising from the table, the students can practise in groups (of four or five), enacting a situation where a host or hostess (or host *and* hostess) are welcoming guests and offering them something to drink. The guests can either accept, or refuse (and add a reason for refusing).

Exercise 2: The students should actually use a pen and paper in this exercise and write down the name and address as dictated. The stress used by the ticket inspector in the question was determined by what he said before. In practising the dialogue the students should use the contracted form: 'What's your name, sir?' This is a useful exercise for giving spelling practice; a simple skill, but one which sometimes proves a challenge even for fairly advanced students. The 'officials' should write down exactly what they hear, and then check it with the person who dictated it.

In Your Own Words

Re-enact the sketch in your own words, without reading from the text. Do it in short sections. These words will remind you:

Two chairs facing one another will represent the compartment very well. The passenger should have a newspaper (or magazine or book), and the ticket inspector should have a pencil and small notebook (a piece of folded paper will represent this adequately if no small notebooks are to hand) which he keeps in his pocket until the appropriate moment at the beginning of section III. The students should be encouraged to mime the opening and closing of the door, glancing out of the window to see if the train is approaching a station, getting out of the train at the end, and so on. For a more elaborate 'performance' than simple classroom re-enacting, a peaked hat and uniform jacket are needed for the ticket inspector, a tray for the steward, and a cloth over the arm for the waiter.

* Further Role-playing Activities

1 Talking to the Steward and the Waiter

In the sketch, the passenger refused coffee and dinner. (He said 'No, thanks' to the steward and the waiter.) The students can improvise dialogues in pairs, imagining that the passenger did not refuse, but bought something from the steward and made some enquiries of the waiter, as follows:

1 *Passenger and steward*
Buy a coffee. Ask what sandwiches there are. Choose one. Pay. Ask what time the train arrives at its destination.

2 *Passenger and waiter*
Ask what time dinner is served until. Ask how much it costs. Ask what is on the menu. Ask if the train is on time.

2 Situations Parallel to the Sketch

Present these situations to the students:

1 A policeman stops a car. The driver has no licence.
2 An immigration official is talking to a traveller. The traveller has no passport.
3 A theatre manager is talking to a theatre-goer. The theatre-goer has no ticket.

In pairs, the students improvise the conversations, following a similar development to the Ticket Inspector sketch and changing it to incorporate their own ideas. They may then show their results to the class by performing their own sketch, if they would like to, or write their version and present it to another group for 'performing'.

3 Saying What Happened

The students can imagine the situation after the man has left the train, and improvise conversations in either of these ways:

1 The man meets a friend at the station, and tells him about the events on the train.
2 The ticket inspector has a cup of tea in the buffet, and tells the steward and waiter about the events.

Pronunciation Practice

1 Explaining Clearly (Stress)

Replay the tape of the sketch, for the students to identify parts where the ticket inspector is being painstaking in his explanations, and using heavy stresses in doing so.

e.g. 'No, sir. I mean: This is a *first-class* compartment.'
'Not *now*, sir. At the next station.'

Practise similar uses of stress in clarifying, for example, words that sound the same:

e.g. S1: Sorry, did you say 'bush'?
S2: No, not *'bush'* – *'push'*.

2 Surprise (Intonation)

Ask the students to find examples of surprise in the ticket inspector's voice.

e.g. 'Mine?' 'Me, sir?' 'OK?'

Extend this into Question-and-Answer practice, with questions that elicit a surprised response:

e.g. 'I found a hundred pounds in the street.'
– 'A hundred pounds?'

First give some examples yourself, and then allow the students to invent their own.

Writing

Regulations

The ticket inspector mentioned 'the book' – the book of regulations about railway passengers. In the book, there are regulations like this:

Passengers must have a valid ticket.

Write ten more regulations, using these patterns:

Passengers must (not) . . . .
If passengers . . . ., they must . . . .

The students can suggest a few regulations orally in class, and then write them in class or for homework. (This exercise makes a good homework assignment, because it allows for some imagination within a controlled framework.) The regulations can, of course, be serious or humorous, and if they wish, the students can use other patterns, such as 'Passengers are not permitted to . . .' or '-ing is forbidden'.

What Do You Think?

Jobs

In pairs, take the parts of (a) a ticket inspector, a traffic policeman or a park-keeper, (b) an interviewer.

If (a), decide on five good things and five bad things about your job. If (b), think of five questions to ask (a) about their job. Then ask and answer. Then discuss what makes a job interesting, and what your ideal job is.

* This activity can be done in pairs (different pairs should work on different jobs to provide variety). It can also be done in groups of four or five, with one person in each group taking the part of the ticket inspector/traffic policeman/park-keeper and the others being interviewers. If the students are adults, the jobs can be their own jobs. After the work in pairs or in groups, the class can discuss the advantages and disadvantages of different jobs.

2

Gussett and Rose

This sketch began as a dialogue written for the Belgian teaching magazine 'English Pages'. The idea was to have a dialogue which *ended* with the words 'How do you do?' rather than beginning with them. It was then re-written for the stage-show, and used as a link between two other sketches. It was so successful that it became a sketch in its own right. *Gussett and Rose* was first performed in July 1975.
This sketch is suitable for Elementary students and above.

Attitudes and Functions
Surprise
Goodness me!
Well I never!

Correcting
I'm Albert Gussett, as a matter of fact.
No, no, Gloria, actually.

Contradicting
We were in the army together.
– We weren't.

Finding Out
Are you interested in boxing?

Structure and Usage
Main Point
Question forms
e.g. Do you remember that awful teacher?
Are you interested in boxing?

Other Points
Simple Past of 'to be'
e.g. We were in the army together.
We weren't at school together.

Note the Following Words and Expressions
Goodness me! Well I never! It's a small world.
Doesn't time fly! I was wondering about that myself.

Suggested Preliminary Practice
The main item is 'Finding out' and the language we use to find out about people. A good preparation would be a game of Twenty Questions. A student should 'become' a famous person, and the others have to guess who he is. The other students should address the 'famous person' as 'you', so the Question forms being practised will be: 'Do you (live in Europe)?' 'Are you (an actor)?' rather than 'Does he . . . ?' and 'Is he . . . ?'
If no practice is required, introduce the sketch when you are teaching your class the English you need when meeting people.

Preliminary Questions
1 What were the two men's names?
2 Were they both married?
3 When did they first meet?

2

Gussett and Rose

SCENE A street

CHARACTERS Two Englishmen: Albert Gussett and Harold Rose

I *Two men pass in the street.*

ROSE Goodness me!

GUSSETT Well I never!

ROSE Herbert Bishop!

GUSSETT Arthur Trigwell!

ROSE No . . . actually my name's Harold Rose.

GUSSETT I'm Albert Gussett, as a matter of fact.

ROSE Albert Gussett. Of course.

GUSSETT And you're Harold Rose. Of course you are.

ROSE Well I never!

GUSSETT Goodness me!

They hesitate for a moment.

ROSE Well, how are you, then?

GUSSETT Fine, fine. How's Alice?

ROSE Alice?

GUSSETT Yes, Alice. Your wife's name's Alice, isn't it?

ROSE No, no . . . Gloria, actually.

GUSSETT Oh, yes. Gloria Trigwell.

ROSE Er . . . Rose.

GUSSETT Rose Trigwell?

ROSE No. Gloria Rose.

GUSSETT Gloria Rose. Of course. How is she?

ROSE She's very well. How's . . . er . . .

GUSSETT Doris?

ROSE Yes, Doris, your wife. How is she?

GUSSETT She's very well –

ROSE Good, good.

GUSSETT – but she isn't my wife.

ROSE No?

GUSSETT I'm not married.

ROSE Oh.

GUSSETT Doris is my sister.

ROSE Oh, yes.

They hesitate again for a moment.

II Well, it *is* a small world, isn't it, Herbert?

GUSSETT Albert.

ROSE Albert, yes. It seems like yesterday –

GUSSETT Yes, it certainly does . . .

ROSE – when we were at that awful school together.

GUSSETT School?

ROSE Yes. Doesn't time fly?

GUSSETT We weren't at school together.

ROSE Do you remember that awful English teacher with black teeth?

GUSSETT We *weren't* at school together.

ROSE Weren't we?

GUSSETT No, we were in the Army together.

ROSE We weren't.

GUSSETT Weren't we?

ROSE I was in the Navy.

GUSSETT Oh.

They hesitate again for a moment.

III ROSE Er . . . Albert, I mean *Herbert* –

GUSSETT No, no, Albert's my name.

ROSE Er, yes . . . Albert, how *do* we know each other?

GUSSETT I was just wondering about that myself, er . . .

ROSE	Harold.
GUSSETT	Yes, Harold. Are you an architect?
ROSE	Yes! Are *you* an architect?
GUSSETT	No, I'm a taxi-driver.
ROSE	Oh.
	They hesitate again.
GUSSETT	Are you interested in boxing?
ROSE	No, not at all.
GUSSETT	Ah.
ROSE	Do you go to the theatre?
GUSSETT	I went once – about twenty years ago.
ROSE	I see.
GUSSETT	Do you take your holidays in Brighton?
ROSE	No, never.
GUSSETT	Mmm.
ROSE	Do you play golf?
GUSSETT	No, I don't.
ROSE	Well, that's not it then.
	They hesitate again.
IV	Do you know, Albert, I don't think we've met before.
GUSSETT	No, you're right. We haven't.
ROSE	Well, er . . . I'm Harold Rose.
GUSSETT	And I'm Albert Gussett.
ROSE	How do you do?
GUSSETT	How do you do?
	They shake hands.

Listening Comprehension

Questions

I 1 How did the two men feel when they met each other?
2 Who are Gloria and Doris?
II 3 Did the two men go to the same school?
4 Who had been in the Army and who had been in the Navy?
III 5 What was Albert Gussett's job?
6 Did both men like playing golf?
IV 7 Did they have anything in common?
8 Was this their first meeting?

For Questions 2, 4 and 5, which concern small details, you may like to let the students listen several times to the relevant parts of the sketch, or refer to the text. The other questions are more general, and can be answered following the listening to the sketch.

*Reading Comprehension

Read and Re-tell

Read the story, and then re-tell it.

A young man went to work for the British diplomatic service in India. Twenty years later, he returned to England. Everything was completely different. After a few days, he was invited to go to a party. He arrived, feeling rather lost and lonely. Suddenly, he saw a face that he recognized – a lady he used to know when he was younger. He rushed across the room.

'Hello, how are you?' he said, smiling.

The lady looked at him blankly.

'I've just come back from India,' he said, still smiling. 'Been there twenty years.'

'Have you?' said the lady, puzzled.

'Yes,' said the man, beginning to feel rather uncomfortable. 'Er . . . how's your sister, by the way?'

'Oh, she's very well,' said the lady, surprised. 'She's still the Queen.'

Put the students in pairs and let them read the story silently. Then one student should re-tell the story to the other. The second student can correct him. After this activity, you may like to tell the story to the whole class, making deliberate mistakes tongue-in-cheek so that the class correct you.

Word Puzzle

There are a lot of *names* in the sketch, including a few wrong ones! Read the sketch again, fill in the names, and find the word in the box. Be careful – Number 5 is different from the others.

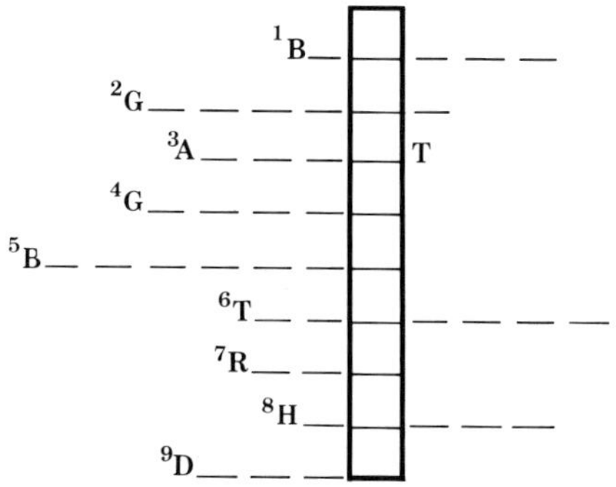

Solution: 1 Bishop 2 Gussett 3 Albert 4 Gloria 5 Brighton 6 Trigwell 7 Rose 8 Harold 9 Doris. The word in the vertical box is 'strangers' – what Gussett and Rose were.

Communicating

1 *Meeting by Accident*

Gussett and Rose said:

Goodness me! Well I never!

You can practise with:

What a surprise to see you! I can't believe it! What on earth are you doing here? I wasn't expecting to see *you* here!

2 *Finding Common Interests*

Gussett and Rose said:

Are you interested in boxing? – No, not at all. Do you take your holidays in Brighton? – No, never.

They did not find any common interests. But if you do have common interests, you can show it like this:

Do you like skiing?	Yes, quite a lot. Yes, I love it. Yes, I'm very keen on skiing.

Have you been to Paris?	Yes, lots of times. Yes, once or twice. I went last year for the first time.

If not, then:

Do you like	collecting stamps? climbing mountains? Shakespeare? classical music?	No, not much. Not very much. Not really. No, not at all. Not any more. Not these days.

Exercise 1: Gussett and Rose used rather exaggerated phrases but the ones suggested for the students to practice are more usual.
Exercise 2: The students should practise finding common interests in pairs or groups, either using the examples provided or inventing their own real questions.

In Your Own Words

Re-enact the sketch in your own words, without reading from the text. Do it in short sections. These words will remind you:

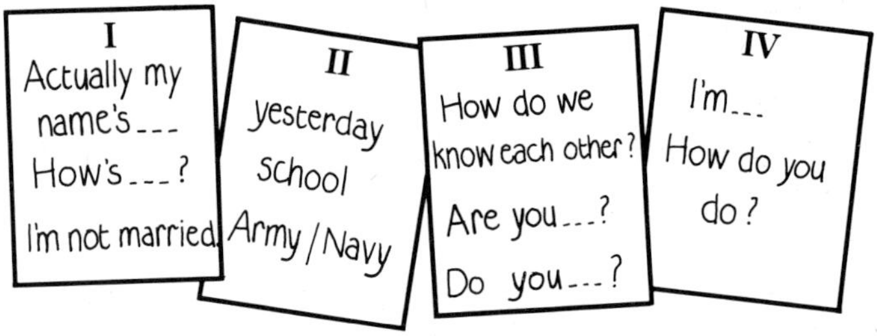

This sketch needs no props at all. The students can, of course, change the names, personal details, questions, etc. as they like. In this sketch in particular, they should not be preoccupied with specific details from the original text.

* Further Role-playing Activities

Meeting and Introducing People

1 The students should practise this in threes. One student introduces two others to each other. The following dialogue should form the basis of the activity:

A : Do you know Paul?
B : No, I don't think we've met before.
C : You're right. I don't think we have.
A : Well, James, this is Paul Jones . . . and Paul, this is James Smith.
B : How do you do?
C : How do you do?

2 Prepare for the same activity as in (1), by devising cue-cards so that the students know details about the character they are playing. The 'host' who will introduce them to each other is given details which are incorrect, so that the other two students will have to correct the introductions.
Here are two examples of what the cards should look like:

1	HOST'S CARD		2
Albert Smith Born in Liverpool, living in Manchester retired teacher climbing mountains	Arthur Smith Liverpool teacher climbing mountains ←	Doris Brown Birmingham doctor swimming →	Dora Brown Birmingham nurse skiing

1	HOST'S CARD		2
Albert Stone Manchester professor walking	Arthur Smith Liverpool teacher climbing mountains ←	Doris Brown Birmingham doctor swimming →	Dora Green Coventry nurse skiing

Pronunciation Practice

Correcting and Contradicting

1 Play one of the parts of the tape where Gussett and Rose correct each other. Let the students practise the intonation.

e.g. We weren't at school together.
- Weren't we?
No, we were in the Army together.
- We weren't.
Weren't we?

2 You can extend the practice of the intonation-pattern, using different examples, the students should think of their own, if possible: the year or month of a visit to England, the address of a friend, the score in a football match, birthdays, and so on. Here is an example:

A : Fred's birthday isn't the 16th of February.
B : Isn't it?
A : No, it's the 12th of March.
B : It isn't.
A : Isn't it?

Writing

Notes for a Biography

Read the sketch very carefully, and write down everything you can find out about Albert Gussett and Harold Rose.
Make *notes* about their jobs, families and hobbies. Then use your notes to write a biography of each man.

Begin the activity orally: go through Part I of the sketch with the students, noting on the blackboard the first facts that occur (the full names of the two men, their marital status, the fact that Albert Gussett has a sister) in two columns. Then allow the students to continue, making their own notes by referring to the text in front of them.

What do You Think?

Strangers

Gussett and Rose were very uncomfortable when they realized that they were strangers. It is said that the English never speak to strangers on buses, in trains, in cafés, etc. Do you think this is a bad thing? Do you talk to strangers when you have the chance? Where?

*For this discussion, the students could work in groups, with each group assigned a particular situation (e.g. group 1 – a café, group 2 – a crowded bus, group 3 – a railway compartment, etc.). Each group could discuss questions like: Do people talk to strangers in this situation? If not, why not? Would the individuals in the group talk to strangers in this situation? The groups could later report back to the whole class and share their findings. Alternatively, the groups could act the roles of strangers in the different situations, and attempt to start a conversation.

3

Yoga for Beginners

As a lot of people study with the aid of cassettes these days, we liked the idea of a cassette which didn't just give information and instructions, but also entered into conversation with the student, got offended, answered back, persuaded, cajoled and so on; and was generally 'human'. A course of yoga for beginners seemed a suitable context for this to happen in! The sketch was first performed in July 1975. At the end of the stage version, the lights faded to black as the batteries in the cassette-recorder ran down and the student called for help.

This sketch can be used with Elementary students, providing the vocabulary is practised beforehand (see Words and Expressions) and that the Present Perfect is treated idiomatically (see Preliminary Practice).

Attitudes and Functions

Giving Instructions
Do this first exercise on the floor. Cross your legs and straighten your back.
Put your *right* hand under your *left* knee.
Don't touch that button.
You must follow the instructions very carefully.

Carrying out Instructions
Right hand . . . right knee . . . right foot. Yes. I've done that.

Persuading
Now, come along.
Let's try again.
– Why?
Well, because yoga is good for you.

Surprise
What?!
What do you mean: 'Don't touch that button'?

Structure and Usage

Main Point
Positive and Negative Imperatives
e.g. Cross your legs and straighten your back.
Don't touch that button.

Other Points
'Must'
e.g. Every part of your body must relax.
You must follow these instructions very carefully.
Present Simple tense
e.g. What do you mean?
Everybody does it: doctors do it . . .
Present Perfect tense
e.g. I've done that./I've done it! (See *Note* below)

Note the Following Words and Expressions

Connected with tape-recorders: Play Stop Fast forward Rewind button battery/ies
Connected with bodily movement: hold touch straighten keep . . . straight cross (legs) body knee back
Other expressions: I've done it! Come along. (It's) good for you.

Suggested Preliminary Practice

Note: The Present Perfect tense only occurs in two First Person examples ('I've done that' and 'I've done it!'), and these can be treated 'idiomatically'; the sketch can thus be used with quite elementary students.

Preliminary practice should focus on the giving and carrying out of instructions. Here are two suggestions:

A *Having a photograph taken*. In pairs, the students take the roles of a photographer and a person being photographed. The 'photographer' tells the 'customer' how to sit or stand ('Sit there', 'Cross your legs', 'Look this way', 'Hold this vase of flowers', etc.), and the 'customer' follows the instructions until finally the photograph is taken. Give an example for the whole class first, and then let the students work in pairs.

B *Operating a tape-recorder*. Draw a simple diagram of a tape-recorder on the blackboard, with the buttons clearly marked. For example:

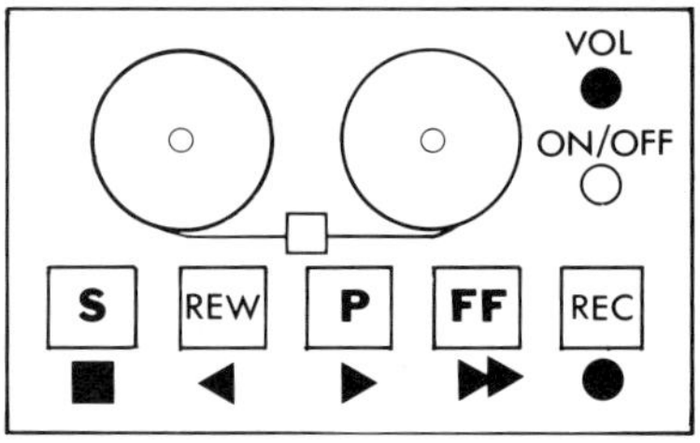

Then, first ask the students what the letters on the buttons mean, and follow this with prompt sentences which will elicit instructions:

I want to play the tape.	→ Press the 'Play' button.
I want to stop the tape.	→ Press the 'Stop' button.
I want to go back.	→ Press the 'Rewind' button.
I want to go forward.	→ Press the 'Fast forward' button.
I want to record.	→ Press the 'Record' button.

Preliminary Questions

1 Was the woman studying yoga in a class?
2 What was special about the cassette?
3 Did she finish the lesson?

3

Yoga for Beginners

SCENE	A room in the woman's house
CHARACTERS	A woman who is studying yoga The voice on a cassette

I WOMAN — Right.

She puts her cassette-player on a table, and checks it.

Play. Stop. Fast forward. Stop. Rewind. Stop. Yes, that's O.K. Now . . .

She finds the cassette.

. . . ah, yes, here it is. 'Yoga for Beginners'. Good.

She puts the cassette into the cassette-player.

Now. Play.

She starts the cassette.

VOICE — 'Yoga for Beginners'. Lesson 1, Part 1, Unit 1, Section 1, Paragraph 1: *One*. Do this first exercise on the floor. *Sit* on the floor.

The woman follows the instructions.

Cross your legs and straighten your back. Now relax. Relax. Every part of your body must *relax*.

The woman falls over.

Hmm. Now sit up again. Straighten your back and relax. But keep your back straight.

The woman does this.

II Good. Lesson 1, Part 1, Unit 1, Section 1, Paragraph 1: *Two*. Now touch your right knee –

WOMAN Oh, that's easy.

The woman touches her right knee.

VOICE – with your head. But keep your back straight.

WOMAN Oh. (*Doing it:*) Ow . . . ooh!

VOICE Good. Now put your *right* hand under your *left* knee, and hold your *right* foot.

WOMAN Right hand . . . left knee . . . right foot. I've done that.

VOICE Good. Now, put your *left* hand under your *right* knee, and hold your *left* foot.

WOMAN Left hand . . . right knee . . . left foot. Yes, I've done that.

VOICE And keep your back straight.

WOMAN Oh.

She tries to do this, and falls over again.

Aaaargh!

VOICE Now sit up again and relax. Good. Lesson 1, Part 1, Unit 1, Section 1, Paragraph 1: *Three*. Put your *right* hand under your *right* knee, and hold your *right* foot.

WOMAN Oh, dear. Right hand . . . right knee . . . right foot. Yes, I've done that.

VOICE Good. Now put your *left* hand under your *left* knee, and hold your *left* foot.

The woman tries to do this.

WOMAN I can't do it.

VOICE Now, come along. Put your *left* hand under your *left* knee, and hold your *left* foot.

The woman tries again.

WOMAN I can't do it.

She stands up and walks across to the table.

III No more yoga for me.

VOICE Don't touch that button!

WOMAN What?!

VOICE Don't touch that button!

WOMAN What do you mean: 'Don't touch that button'?

VOICE Don't touch it.

WOMAN Don't talk to me like that.

VOICE Don't touch that button . . . *please*.

WOMAN That's better.

VOICE — Let's try again.

WOMAN — It's too difficult.

VOICE — No, it isn't. Let's try again.

WOMAN — Why?

VOICE — Well, because yoga is good for you.

WOMAN — Good for you?

VOICE — Yes. Everybody does it: doctors do it . . .

WOMAN — (*Not interested:*) Really?

VOICE — . . . university professors do it . . .

WOMAN — (*Not interested:*) Really?

VOICE — . . . and famous actresses and film stars do it.

WOMAN — (*Interested:*) Really? Oh, well . . . O.K.

She sits on the floor again.

IV — Now . . . right hand under right knee . . . hold right foot. Yes, I've done that.

VOICE — Good. Now put your *left* hand under your *left* knee, and hold your *left* foot.

WOMAN — Left hand . . . left knee . . . left foot. I've done it!

VOICE — Good. That position is Position One. Now: Instructions for getting *out* of Position One. Getting out of Position One is not very difficult. But you must follow the instructions very carefully.

The tape begins to slow down.

First . . . take . . . your . . . left . . . hand . . .

WOMAN — Oh, no! The batteries! Um . . . quick! Hurry up! . . . Help! Help!

Listening Comprehension

Questions

I 1 Was the woman standing up for the first exercise?
2 Was the first exercise easy?
II 3 Did the woman do the second exercise?
4 What happened at the end of the second exercise?
5 Why did the woman want to stop the lesson?
III 6 Did the cassette say anything unusual?
7 What kind of people did the cassette mention?
8 Why did the woman continue the lesson?
IV 9 What was wrong with the cassette-player?
10 Why did the woman shout 'Help!'?

In answering Question 2, the students should say *what* the first exercise was ('The woman sat on the floor, crossed her legs, straightened her back and relaxed') as this shows *why* it was easy. For Question 6, the students can listen again and point out the sentences which were unusual in sections I and II ('Now sit up again', 'Now come along'), as well as section III, which is all unusual. In answering Question 9, you may have to give the students the word 'weak' ('The batteries were weak'), or 'run down' ('The batteries were running down'), or 'run out' ('The batteries were running out').

Reading Comprehension

Where Could You Read This?

Read these instructions and say where they come from.

1
Place in boiling water.
Boil for ten minutes.
Serve hot.

2
Write in ink.
Use BLOCK CAPITALS.
Put the date and your signature at the bottom.

3
Dissolve one tablet in a little water.
Repeat the dose every three hours.
Maximum: Eight doses in 24 hours.

4
Do not feed the animals.
Keep away from the bars.

5
Lift receiver and wait for dialling tone.
Dial number.
Insert coin or coins.
(Repeat for more time.)

In pairs or groups, the students read the instructions and decide where they would be found. 1. A can or packet of food 2. A form 3. A bottle or packet of medicine 4. A cage in a zoo 5. A public telephone. They should note down their decisions for the five items. Then, with the class as a whole, the groups can say what they decided and why. At this point you can also deal with new words and expressions, and comment on any other points, for example, the possible ambiguity in the word 'bars' (No. 4), and the missing articles in No. 5.

Word Puzzle

Look at this diagram of a cassette recorder. What are the numbered parts? Write the words in the horizontal boxes. The letters in the vertical box will spell a word.

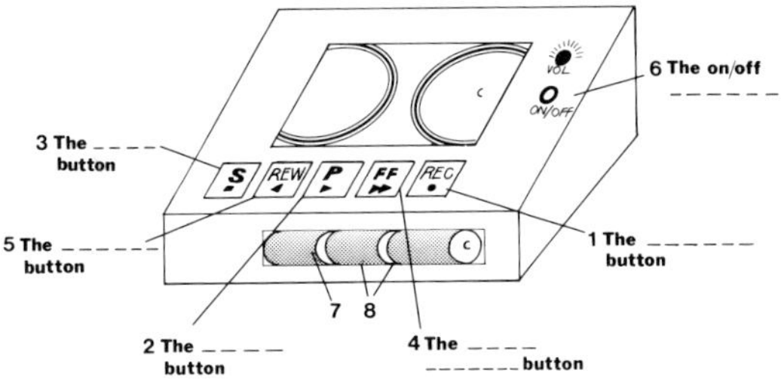

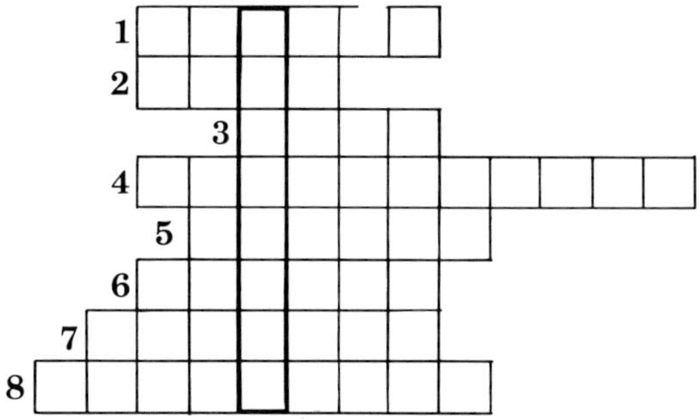

Solution: 1 Record 2 Play 3 Stop 4 Fast forward 5 Rewind 6 button 7 battery 8 batteries. The letters in the vertical box thus spell 'cassette'.

Communicating

1 *Giving and Following Instructions*

The cassette gave the woman instructions. For example:

> Put your right hand under your right knee, and hold your right foot.

The woman followed the instructions. For example:

> Right hand . . . right knee . . . right foot.
> Yes, I've done that.

Practise in pairs, giving and following instructions in the same way. Use these instructions from p. 28:

> Lift receiver and wait for dialling tone.
> Dial number.
> Insert coin or coins. (Repeat for more time.)

2 *Persuading*

The cassette persuaded the woman to continue with yoga:

> – Why?
> – Well, because yoga is good for you. . . . Everybody does it: doctors do it . . . university professors do it . . . and famous actresses and film stars do it.

Listen to that part of the sketch again. Then make similar dialogues about:

riding a bicycle / jogging / meditation

You can use these phrases:

It'll make you	healthy. successful, etc.
If you don't	you'll be . . . . you won't be . . . .

Exercise 1: For this exercise, the students should imagine that they are in a telephone-box, and one student is reading out the instructions while the other carries them out. The first student can add in the missing articles as he gives the instructions; the second student can speak as the woman in the sketch did, repeating the key words and saying 'I've done that' for each action. You may also like to make prompt-cards with other instructions, e.g. working a record-player, opening a safe.

Exercise 2: Play the appropriate section of the sketch again, and then allow the students to practise in pairs. They can, of course, substitute other professions or add other reasons of their own. The student being 'persuaded' can remain unconvinced or become interested (as the woman in the sketch did).

In Your Own Words

Re-enact the sketch in your own words, without reading from the text. Do it in short sections. These words will remind you:

Re-enacting this sketch may not appeal to everyone. Obviously, the students do not have to go through all the same movements as the woman in the sketch. They can approximate them or substitute others which involve fewer contortions! In simple classroom re-enacting in pairs, boxes or even books can be used to represent the cassette-player and should be held by the student who has taken the role of the cassette voice.

* Further Role-playing Activities

1 Photographer and Customers

This activity is a slightly more elaborate form of the one suggested for Preliminary Practice (p. 24).

Divide the students into threes: a 'photographer' and two 'customers', and give the 'customers' roles. For example:

– a bride and groom
– a pop singer and his/her manager
– the finalists in a tennis tournament
– two politicians

The 'photographer' should give the 'customers' instructions on how to sit or stand, choosing appropriate poses for the specific 'customers'. For example, the 'politicians' could be told to shake hands, the tennis players to hold up the cup, and so on. They should follow the instructions until the photograph is taken. (You may like to give the 'photographers' expressions like 'Hold it', 'Say "Cheese"' or 'Now – a nice big smile' for the moment when the photograph is taken.)

2 A Guessing Game

On slips of paper, write the names of jobs which can be easily mimed, for example: waiter, traffic policeman, lift attendant. With the students in pairs, give a slip of paper to one student. This student must then give instructions to the other on how to stand and move (e.g. 'Pick up a tray. Put some plates on it. Carry the tray to a table. Put the plates on the table. Smile . . .'). The second student carries out the instructions in mime, and he, or the rest of the class, should try to guess the job which is being mimed.

This can also be played as a team game. A member of one team gives instructions to a member of the other team. If the instructions are clear enough for the other members of the first team to guess the job, the first team gets a point.

Pronunciation Practice

Intonation

A Replay the last ten lines of section III of the sketch, and draw the students' attention to the way the woman says 'Really?' Ask them what the difference is: Are all three the same? Are all three different? They should identify the lack of interest in the first two examples, and the interest in the third.
Then, ask the students to say:
1 Hello
– to someone they meet every day
– to an old friend they haven't seen for a long time
2 Thank you
– to a bus conductor who gives them a ticket
– to someone who gives them a fantastic birthday present

B Play section II of the sketch again, and ask the students to say how many times the woman says 'I've done that'. (There are three examples.) Then play section IV, and ask them to do the same. (There is one example, and she also says 'I've done it!') Discuss the difference between the woman's feelings when she says 'I've done that' and when she says 'I've done it!' In the first case, she is matter-of-fact, and in the second she is very pleased with her success.

Writing

Instructions in a Handbook

This is the first page of the woman's 'Yoga for Beginners' handbook:

YOGA FOR BEGINNERS: LESSON 1
Part 1
Unit 1
Section 1
Paragraph 1

1: Do this first exercise on the floor. *Sit* on the floor. Cross your legs and straighten your back. Now relax. Every part of your body must relax. Now sit up again. Straighten your back and relax . . . but keep your back straight.
2: . . . .
3: . . . .
4: . . . .

Listen to the sketch again, and write exercises 2 and 3. Then add a fourth exercise of your own.

Play section I of the sketch while the students follow the lines from the 'handbook' above. Then play section II, so that the students can make notes about the second and third exercises. They should then write up their notes as a continuation of the 'handbook', adding an invented fourth exercise of their own. This can be done individually, in pairs or in groups in the class; alternatively, once the notes have been made for 2 and 3, it can be done for homework.

What Do You Think?

Learning

What is the best way to learn: to learn a language, for example?
In a class with a teacher? At home with a cassette? By watching TV? With a loudspeaker under your pillow while you sleep?

*The students can discuss this question in groups. Firstly, different groups could take one of the methods each, and discuss its advantages and disadvantages. Then the groups could report back to the class as a whole on their findings. The groups could then discuss which method they prefer, and talk about their experiences of learning different things by different methods.

4

Mr Jones

When someone suggested that we write a sketch illustrating the use of 'So do I' and 'Nor do I', we hit on the idea of three men who all claimed to be the same person. Why would they do this? The answer seemed clear: money! The sketch was first performed in July 1975, and has been televised in Portugal and Holland. For this book, the ending has been slightly altered: in the stage version, Mr Jones and his cousin Jane celebrated their good fortune with a song!
This sketch is suitable for Intermediate students and can also be used with Elementary students providing the teacher is aware that a few Relative clauses occur in the sketch and is prepared to comment on them as necessary.

Attitudes and Functions

Disbelief
You don't! You haven't got a Welsh accent.
You haven't! What are they called?

Misunderstanding
I didn't understand the advertisement.
I didn't realize it meant Charles *Edward* Jones.

Apologizing
Sorry to have troubled you.

Contradicting
You're a rich man.
– I'm not.

Explaining Clearly
You're *half* a millionaire.
No, no, no. You share the money with one other relation.

Structure and Usage

Main Point
'So (do I)'/'Nor (do I)'
e.g. I come from Cardiff. – So do I.
My name isn't Jones. – Nor is mine.

Other Points
Relative clauses
e.g. The Mr Jones I want to see has got three children.
Mr Charles Edward Jones, who lives in Cardiff . . .
He's the man you're looking for.

Note the Following Words and Expressions

advertisement Welsh accent tax realize millionaire celebrate share What a coincidence! as a matter of fact (you've) grown up.

Suggested Preliminary Practice

Practise 'So do I'/'Nor do I' via the subject of likes and dislikes. This can be done effectively as a game, either with the class as a whole or in groups of six or eight students. Student A starts with a statement (e.g. 'I like skiing'), with which Student B agrees ('So do I'). Student B then continues with a statement about something he/she dislikes (e.g. 'I don't like snakes'), with which Student C agrees ('Nor do I'). This 'chain' continues round the students. While this is going on, all the students make notes, so that at the end of the 'chain' they can describe the likes and dislikes of any student in the class. (The 'chain' should not progress too fast, and brief pauses can be incorporated if necessary.)

Preliminary Questions

1 Who were the three men?
2 Why did they come to see the girl?
3 Did Mr Jones receive good news or bad news?

4

Mr Jones

SCENE — An office, at four o'clock one afternoon

CHARACTERS — A girl
Mr Charles Jones
'Mr Jones' No. 2
'Mr Jones' No. 3

I *Mr Jones goes into an office.*

MR JONES Good afternoon.

GIRL Good afternoon.

MR JONES My name's Jones. Charles Jones. I come from Wales, from Cardiff. I saw an advertisement in the newspaper. It said: 'Charles Jones. Money. Four o'clock. Tuesday afternoon.' And it gave this address.

GIRL Ah yes. Wait in here please, Mr Jones.

She takes Mr Jones into another office.

MR JONES Thank you.

GIRL With these two gentlemen.

MR JONES Oh, thank you.

The girl goes out.

MR JONES Good afternoon.

MR JONES 2 Good afternoon.

MR JONES Good afternoon.

MR JONES 3 Good afternoon.

MR JONES Nice day, isn't it?

MR JONES 2 Yes.

MR JONES 3 Yes, it is.

II *The girl comes in.*

GIRL Now – Mr Jones?

MR JONES
MR JONES 2 } Yes?
MR JONES 3

GIRL Mr *Jones*.

MR JONES
MR JONES 2 } Yes?
MR JONES 3

GIRL Which one of you is Mr Jones?

MR JONES I am.

MR JONES 2 So am I.

MR JONES 3 So am I.

MR JONES No, *my* name's Jones.

MR JONES 2 So's mine.

MR JONES 3 So's mine.

GIRL I want to speak to Mr *Charles* Jones.

MR JONES Charles Jones! That's me!

MR JONES 2 No, *I'm* Charles Jones.

MR JONES 3 That's my name, too!

GIRL Charles *Edward* Jones.

MR JONES Yes! My name is Charles Edward Jones.

MR JONES 3 So's mine.

MR JONES 2 Mine is, too!

GIRL I want to speak to Mr Charles Edward Jones from Cardiff.

MR JONES That's right. *I* come from Cardiff.

MR JONES 2 (*In a Welsh accent:*) So do I.

MR JONES 3 So do I.

MR JONES You don't! You haven't got a Welsh accent.

MR JONES 3 I know. I went to a good school.

GIRL The Mr Jones I want to see has got three children.

MR JONES Yes, that's me! I've got three children.

	MR JONES 3	So have I.
		The other man hesitates.
	GIRL	What about you?
	MR JONES 2	I've got three children.
	MR JONES	You haven't! What are they called?
	MR JONES 2	What are *yours* called?
	MR JONES	Alan, Michael and David.
	MR JONES 2	So are mine.
	MR JONES 3	What a coincidence! So are mine.
	GIRL	So you *all* say you're Mr Jones?
	MR JONES MR JONES 2 MR JONES 3	Yes.
	GIRL	And you *all* saw the advertisement in the newspaper.
	MR JONES MR JONES 2 MR JONES 3	Yes.
	GIRL	(*Very seriously:*) Well, Mr Charles Edward Jones, who lives in Cardiff, and has three children, hasn't paid any tax for the last five years. He must pay the government *five thousand pounds.*
III	MR JONES 2	Er . . . actually, my name *isn't* Jones.
	MR JONES 3	Nor is mine, and I don't live in Cardiff, either.
	MR JONES 2	Nor do I. I live in . . . Edinburgh, as a matter of fact. I didn't understand the advertisement.
	MR JONES 3	Nor did I. I didn't realize it meant Charles *Edward* Jones.
	MR JONES 2	Nor did I. My name isn't Charles *Edward* Jones.
	MR JONES 3	Nor is mine. *He's* the man you're looking for.
	MR JONES	Oh dear.
	MR JONES 2	Yes, of course he is! Sorry to have troubled you. Goodbye.
	MR JONES 3	Yes, sorry to have troubled you. Goodbye.
		The two men leave.
IV	GIRL	So you're Mr Jones.
	MR JONES	Yes.
	GIRL	Congratulations.
	MR JONES	Eh?
	GIRL	You're a rich man.
	MR JONES	I'm not!
	GIRL	Yes, you are. You've got a lot of money!
	MR JONES	I haven't. I can't pay that tax.
	GIRL	There isn't any tax!
	MR JONES	I haven't got – No tax?
	GIRL	No. That was just a story. I had to find the *real* Mr Jones.
	MR JONES	Why?
	GIRL	Because the real Mr Jones is a very rich man.

MR JONES	I don't understand.
GIRL	Mr Jones – Charlie – Your great-uncle Max died last week.
MR JONES	Oh, no . . .
GIRL	And his money goes to you!
MR JONES	To me? But great-uncle Max was a millionaire!
GIRL	That's right.
MR JONES	So now *I'm* a millionaire?
GIRL	Er . . . no.
MR JONES	Oh.
GIRL	You're *half* a millionaire.
MR JONES	Half a millionaire? Which half? The top half or the bottom half?
GIRL	No, no, no. You share the money with one other relation.
MR JONES	Half a millionaire! Who do I share the money with?
GIRL	Me!
MR JONES	You?
GIRL	Yes, I'm your cousin Jane.
MR JONES	Cousin Jane? Really? *You've* grown up!
GIRL	So have you.
MR JONES	And now you're half a millionaire.
GIRL	And so are you! Let's go out and celebrate.
MR JONES	Good idea! Let's go out and celebrate! Come on!
	He opens the door.
	Oh . . . er . . . Jane?
GIRL	Yes?
MR JONES	Have you got enough money for the bus fare?

Listening Comprehension

Questions

I 1 What did the advertisement in the newspaper say?
2 Where was Mr Jones from?
II 3 What was Mr Jones' full name?
4 How many children did he have?
5 What were Mr Jones' children called?
6 How did the girl explain the advertisement?
III 7 Why did the two men leave?
IV 8 Why did the girl congratulate Mr Jones?
9 Why did she tell the story about the tax?
10 What did Mr Jones and Jane decide to do?

In answering Question 6, the students can give the girl's initial explanation (the tax story), and add whether it was true in the light of the rest of the sketch.

*Reading Comprehension

Advertisements: Read and Explain

Mr Jones read this advertisement in the personal column of a newspaper:

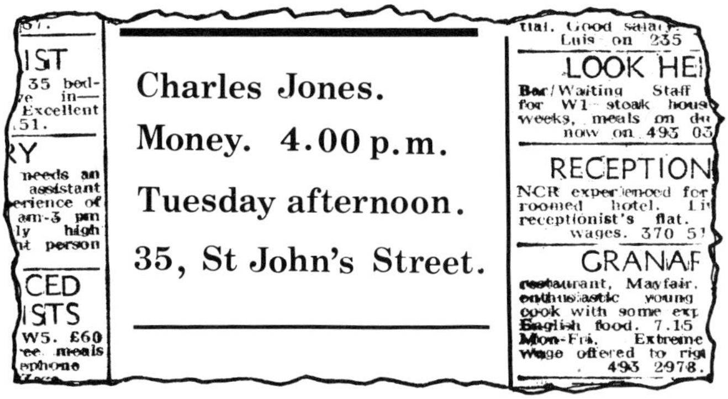

Charles Jones.
Money. 4.00 p.m.
Tuesday afternoon.
35, St John's Street.

These are some more advertisements from the same column. What do they mean?

1 Paul. Desperate. Please ring. Annette.
2 Lost: Diamond necklace. Big reward. Ring 0215-996.
3 Wanted: Anything old. Good prices. Box 27.
4 Lonely? Meet new friends at Tony's. Tuesdays, 8.00 p.m.
5 Young man, 23, needs money. Anything legal considered. Box 28.

Discuss the advertisement which Mr Jones saw with the class as a whole first. Show how the meaning ('Charles Jones should go to 35, St John's Street at four o'clock on . . .') is condensed into a few words. Then the students should read the other advertisements, they can do this in pairs or in groups, and make notes about their interpretation of them. Then, with the class as a whole, these findings can be discussed, and any explanations that are required can be given. As a follow-up activity in class or for homework, the students could write a 'full' version of the message contained in each advertisement, or write a few advertisements in 'telegram language' themselves.

Word Puzzle

Solve the puzzle below, and you'll find the word which describes a man like Mr Jones. It will appear in the diagonal squares.

No. 1 is where Mr Jones comes from.
No. 2 is where he saw the advertisement.
No. 3 describes his great-uncle Max.
No. 4 is the day he had to go to the office.
No. 5 is his first name.
Nos. 6, 7 and 8 are the names of his children.

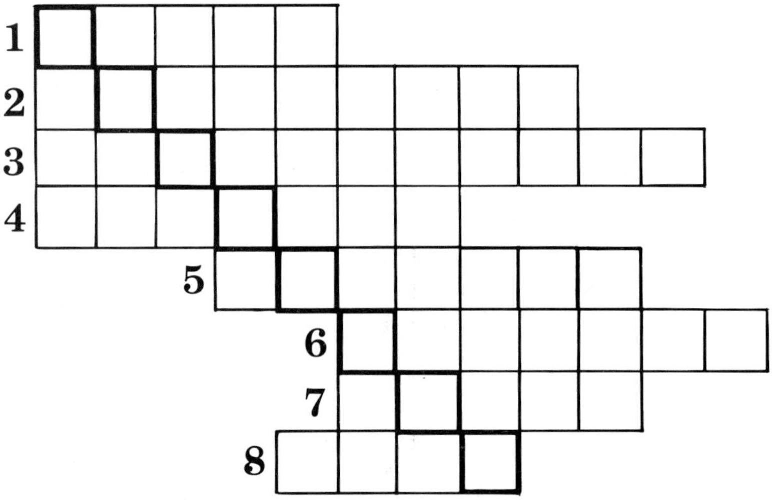

Solution: 1 Wales 2 newspaper 3 millionaire 4 Tuesday 5 Charles 6 Michael 7 David 8 Alan The word in the diagonal squares is thus 'Welshman'.

Communicating

1 Misunderstandings

In the sketch, the two men said that they did not understand the advertisement. They were pretending, but sometimes you really need to show that you didn't understand something, for example, if you want to return something to a shop, or change a ticket after you've bought it. In this situation, you could say:

> I didn't realize what sort it was.
> I thought it was (a return ticket/a cotton shirt).
> I didn't mean to buy one of these.

Practise in pairs:
– taking a shirt back to a shop
– taking a ticket back to a ticket office
– taking a ticket back to a theatre

For example:
'Good morning . . .
I bought this shirt here (yesterday) . . .
I thought it was a . . .
I didn't realize it was a . . .
I'd like to exchange it for a . . .' etc.

2 Apologizing

In the sketch, the two men said:

'Sorry to have troubled you.'

as they left.

Practise apologizing like that. In pairs, make dialogues like this:

A : Good morning. Can I help you?
B : Yes. I'd like to buy *a hat*.
A : I'm sorry. We don't sell *hats*. This is *a bookshop*.
B : Is it really? Sorry to have troubled you. Goodbye.
A : Goodbye.

Put your own words for those in italics.

Before these exercises, play section III of the sketch to the students again, and draw their attention to the appropriate lines.

Exercise 1: The students should complete the model dialogue and then practise in pairs. Cue-cards may be useful, for example:

CLOTHES SHOP You are the shop-assistant.	CLOTHES SHOP You are a customer. You bought a silk shirt by mistake. You wanted a cotton one.

Exercise 2: Practise the dialogue given with the class first, and then allow the students to make their own dialogues in pairs, substituting their own ideas for the words in italics. For example: a suitcase/suitcases/a chemist's; some chairs/chairs/a newsagent's.

In Your Own Words

Re-enact the sketch in your own words, without reading from the text. Do it in short sections. These words will remind you:

For re-enacting this sketch, it is useful if the three men can be seated on chairs side by side, with the real Mr Jones in the middle. The girl can stand or sit slightly apart from them. No 'props' are really vital, although a newspaper for each of the three men is useful, and possibly a pair of glasses, a pen and some papers for the girl, to give her a stern, official appearance in the first three sections.

Further Role-playing Activities

An Alternative Version of the Sketch

Ask the students to think of the situation in the sketch slightly differently: The two other men are in fact called Charles Edward Jones, but they realize very early on that they are not the *right* Charles Edward Jones.

In groups, the students should read the sketch again, and work out what the two men would have said if they had told the truth. The sketch will remain the same as far as the line 'Mine is, too!' in section II, but after that it will become clear who is the right Mr Jones, as they all give the true facts about themselves. Although in reality, she might have stopped earlier, the girl can ask all her questions (home town, number of children, names of children) and all three men can reply. The students should continue up to the point where the two *wrong* 'Mr Joneses' leave.

After they have worked out their versions in their groups, one or more groups may like to 'perform' their version for the rest of the class.

Pronunciation Practice

Disbelief (Intonation)

In the middle of section II of the sketch, Mr Jones challenges the other two men. Replay to the students the lines where he says:

'You don't! You haven't got a Welsh accent.'

and:

'You haven't! What are they called?'

Practise with the students the intonation of 'You don't!' and 'You haven't!' Then get them to respond in the same way to these statements:

– I've met the President.
– I live in a castle.
– I can speak Welsh.
– I'm writing a biography of Napoleon.
– I went to the South Pole for my holidays.

Make sure that the students add a remark after saying 'You haven't!'/'You don't!'/'You can't!'/'You aren't!'/'You didn't!' For example, for the first one, the response might be: 'You haven't! You've only seen him on TV.'

Writing

A Dialogue

When Mr Jones came home, his wife wanted to know what had happened. This is what Mrs Jones said. What did Mr Jones say?

Mrs Jones	Well, dear – good news or bad?
Mr Jones	....
Mrs Jones	What do you mean: 'good *and* bad'?
Mr Jones	....
Mrs Jones	Great-uncle Max? Oh, how sad! What's the *good* news?
Mr Jones	....
Mrs Jones	What – *all* his money?
Mr Jones	....
Mrs Jones	But he was a millionaire, wasn't he?
Mr Jones	....
Mrs Jones	Half a million pounds! Well, we've got to celebrate!
Mr Jones	....
Mrs Jones	What do you mean – you've already celebrated?
Mr Jones	....
Mrs Jones	Jane? Who's Jane?
Mr Jones	....
Mrs Jones	I see. So that's why you're so late.

This exercise can be done in groups. Make sure that the students use the 'clues' in deciding what Mr Jones said. For example, a stressed word is often a good clue to the preceding line ('What do you mean: "good *and* bad"?' 'What – *all* his money?'), and so are obvious repetitions ('Half a million pounds!' 'Jane?'). When the groups have completed their dialogues, pairs from each group can read out their version for the rest of the class to discuss.

What Do You Think?

Money

Charles Jones is a lucky man – he's got half a million pounds to spend. He won't have any problems for the rest of his life. On the other hand, perhaps his problems are just beginning. What do you think?

*In groups, the students can discuss the advantages and disadvantages of suddenly becoming very rich. One member of the group can be appointed to take notes of points made in two lists, points on the positive side and points on the negative side. The groups can then compare their findings. Following that, the groups can continue their discussion by speculating on what they would do if they were in Mr Jones' position.

5

The Customs Officer

The Customs Officer sketch was first performed in July 1977. The stage version is very much the same as the text given here, except that Strogonov had three passports instead of two, and the customs officer tried to open Strogonov's case with a dramatic karate movement! In the show in which the sketch was used, Strogonov actually appeared as a recurrent character in every sketch.
This sketch is suitable for Intermediate students and above.

Attitudes and Functions

Official Politeness
Good morning, sir.
Could I see your passport, please?
Would you mind opening the case please, sir?

Suspicion
This is very strange, sir.
You don't *look* very British . . .
You say your name is Vladimir Strogonov.
It all looks very suspicious.
You haven't come to England to sell these papers, have you?

Astonishment
Nationality: British?!
Occupation: Spy!?
Dynamite?!

Disbelief
A brush salesman?
I see.
A brush?
I don't believe a word of it.

Irritation
No! . . . No! . . . No!!
I'm not interested in your wife.

Explaining Clearly
When I say: 'Have you got anything to declare?' I mean . . .

Structure and Usage

Main Point
It looks (like) . . ./It sounds (like) . . .
e.g. Vladimir Strogonov doesn't *sound* very British.
It looks like a bottle of whisky.
It sounds like a clock.

Polite Question forms
e.g. Could I see your passport, please?
Would you like to buy a new toothbrush?
Would you mind opening the case please, sir?
Have you got . . .?
e.g. Have you got anything to declare?
Have you got any whisky?

Note the Following Words and Expressions

Expressions connected with the customs: passport declare nationality occupation whisky perfume secret spy
Other expressions: spelling mistake suspicious ticking noise alarm-clock attached unlock I can assure you . . . There you are.

Note: 'ticking noise', 'attached' and 'unlock' need not be taught explicitly. They are easily understood from the context.

Suggested Preliminary Practice

Practise or revise the difference between, for example:

'It's a clock.'

and:

'It sounds like a clock.'

Also use objects or visual aids which will provoke practice of 'looks like . . .': for example (a) pictures of objects which are not immediately recognizable ('It looks like a horse.'); (b) objects in wrapping paper ('It looks like a hair-dryer.'); (c) objects in boxes ('It sounds like a spoon.').

If no structure practice is required, introduce the sketch with some practice of the language used at the customs.

Preliminary Questions

1 What was the traveller's name and occupation?
2 What was in his case?
3 Why was he in England?

5

The Customs Officer

SCENE — The customs hall at an airport or port in England

CHARACTERS — A customs officer
Vladimir Strogonov

I OFFICER — Good morning, sir.

STROGONOV — Good morning.

OFFICER — Welcome to England.

STROGONOV — Thank you.

OFFICER — Are you staying long?

STROGONOV — Yes. Er . . . no. Perhaps. I'm not sure.

OFFICER — I see. Could I see your passport, please?

STROGONOV — Yes. Here you are.

OFFICER — Thank you.

Strogonov gives the customs officer a passport. (*Reading from the passport:*) Mrs Elizabeth Robinson?

STROGONOV — Oh, sorry. Try this one.

He gives the customs officer another passport.

OFFICER	This is very strange, sir. Why have you got *two* passports?
STROGONOV	Well, I travel a lot.
OFFICER	I see. Hmm . . . (*Reading from the passport:*) Name: Vladimir Strogonov.
STROGONOV	*Strog*onov.
OFFICER	Pardon?
STROGONOV	*Strog*onov. Vladimir *Strog*onov.
OFFICER	*Strog*onov, yes. Nationality . . . Nationality: British?!
STROGONOV	That's right.
OFFICER	Vladimir Strogonov doesn't *sound* very British.
STROGONOV	Doesn't it?
OFFICER	No – and *you* don't *look* very British, either.
STROGONOV	Don't I?
OFFICER	No, you don't.
STROGONOV	Oh.

II	OFFICER	Name, nationality . . . occupation. Occupation: Spy!?
	STROGONOV	What?
	OFFICER	It says here that you're a spy.
	STROGONOV	Let me see. *He looks at the passport.* Yes, it looks like 'Spy', doesn't it?
	OFFICER	Yes, it does.
	STROGONOV	It's a spelling mistake.
	OFFICER	A spelling mistake? What *is* your job then?
	STROGONOV	I'm a brush salesman.
	OFFICER	A brush salesman?
	STROGONOV	Yes. Would you like to buy a new toothbrush?
	OFFICER	No!
	STROGONOV	A paintbrush?
	OFFICER	No!
	STROGONOV	A hairbrush?
	OFFICER	No!! Now, you say your name is Vladimir Strogonov, and you say you're British. Your passport says you're a spy, and *you* say you're a brush salesman.
	STROGONOV	That's right.
	OFFICER	Well, it all looks very suspicious, doesn't it?
	STROGONOV	Yes, I suppose it does.

III	OFFICER	Now, have you got anything to declare?
	STROGONOV	Yes, I have.
	OFFICER	What?
	STROGONOV	I love my wife.
	OFFICER	I'm not interested in your wife.
	STROGONOV	I'm very pleased to hear it. I can assure you that my wife is not interested in *you* either.

OFFICER — Sir!! When I say: 'Have you got anything to declare?' I mean: 'Have you got any whisky? Have you got any cigarettes? Have you got any wine? Etcetera, etcetera.'

STROGONOV — No. No 'etceteras' at all.

OFFICER — Then what is *that*, in your pocket?

STROGONOV — Where?

OFFICER — *There!*

The customs officer takes a bottle from Mr Strogonov's pocket.

Ah, yes. Now *this* looks like a bottle of whisky to me.

STROGONOV — Yes, it *looks* like a bottle of whisky – but it isn't.

OFFICER — What is it, then?

STROGONOV — It's a bottle of . . . perfume.

OFFICER — I see. I think I'd better take it.

The customs officer puts the bottle in a drawer.

IV

Now – your case.

STROGONOV — My case?

OFFICER — Yes – on the table, please.

STROGONOV — On the table?

OFFICER — Yes.

Mr Strogonov puts his case on the table.

What's that noise?

STROGONOV — What noise?

OFFICER — That *ticking* noise. It's coming from your case.

STROGONOV — Oh, *that* noise.

OFFICER — Yes. It sounds like a clock. Is it a clock, Mr Strogonov? Or is it a bomb?

STROGONOV — It's a brush.

OFFICER — A brush?

STROGONOV — Yes. It's a special new toothbrush with an alarm-clock attached to it.

OFFICER — An alarm-clock?

STROGONOV — Yes. It wakes you up when it's time to clean your teeth.

OFFICER — I don't believe a word of it. Would you mind *opening* the case please, sir?

STROGONOV — I can't.

OFFICER — Why not?

STROGONOV — It's locked.

OFFICER — Well, *un*lock it.

STROGONOV — I've lost the key.

OFFICER — I see. (*He calls to another customs officer:*) George, bring me that hammer, would you? That's right – the large one.

STROGONOV — What?! Hammer? No, no! It's not locked.

He opens the case.

There you are.

V

OFFICER — Thank you, sir. Aha! What is this?

He takes a toothbrush out of the case. There is an alarm-clock attached to it.

STROGONOV You see – a toothbrush with an alarm-clock attached to it.

OFFICER And what is this?

He takes some dynamite out of the case. It is attached to the toothbrush and alarm-clock.

It looks like dynamite.

STROGONOV That's right.

OFFICER Dynamite?!

STROGONOV Yes.

OFFICER What's it for?

STROGONOV Well, if the alarm-clock doesn't work, it blows up. Boom!

OFFICER Blows up?

STROGONOV Yes. Some people can't wake up in the morning.

OFFICER (*Ironically:*) Very interesting.

The customs officer finds some papers in the case.

And what are these papers?

STROGONOV Oh, they're just information about brushes.

OFFICER Let's have a look. These look like secret papers to me. You haven't come to England to sell these papers, have you, Mr Strogonov?

STROGONOV
OFFICER } *Strog*onov.

OFFICER Now come along, Mr Strogonov. Have you come to England to *sell* these secret papers?

STROGONOV Well . . . as a matter of fact . . . yes, I have.

OFFICER (*Very severely:*) I see. Well, in that case, Mr Strogonov . . . (*Suddenly very friendly:*) . . . welcome to England.

STROGONOV Eh?

OFFICER Welcome to England. There's a car waiting for you outside.

STROGONOV Oh. Thank you very much.

OFFICER Goodbye, sir.

STROGONOV Goodbye.

Mr Strogonov leaves.

OFFICER Right. Who's next? Good morning, madam. Welcome to England . . .

Listening Comprehension

Questions

I 1 What was wrong with Strogonov's first passport?
2 Why was the customs officer surprised when he read 'British' in Strogonov's passport?

II 3 How did Strogonov explain the word 'Spy' in his passport?
4 Do you think Strogonov was a brush salesman?

III 5 Why did the customs officer say: 'I'm not interested in your wife.'?
6 Where did the customs officer see the bottle?

IV 7 What happened when Strogonov put his case on the table?
8 How did Strogonov explain the noise?
9 Was Strogonov's case locked?
10 Did the customs officer use the hammer?

V 11 What was the dynamite for?
12 Why was Strogonov surprised at the end?

Most of these questions provoke very straightforward answers, but No. 11 should provoke some discussion – was the dynamite *really* part of a special alarm-clock or not? Students should not stop at the answer given by Strogonov, but add their own interpretation of what he said.

Reading Comprehension

Read and Explain

Look at the lists below. They show the duty-free allowances for EEC and non-EEC visitors to Britain.

EEC PASSPORT HOLDERS	*NON-EEC PASSPORT HOLDERS*
300 cigarettes	200 cigarettes
or	or
150 cigarillos	100 cigarillos
or	or
75 cigars	50 cigars
or	or
400 grammes of tobacco	250 grammes of tobacco
3 litres of table wine	2 litres of table wine
or	or
$1\frac{1}{2}$ litres of spirits	1 litre of spirits

Read the lists and then explain the regulations. Use expressions like:

If you're an EEC passport holder	you're allowed to . . . you can . . . ------------- you're not allowed to . . . you can't . . . you mustn't (etc.) . . .

If necessary, before starting the exercise, check or explain the difference between EEC and non-EEC passport holders.
The students could work first in pairs: one student keeps the book closed, while the other glances down the EEC list and then explains orally what an EEC passport holder is allowed.

The second then opens his book, and does the same with the non-EEC list. As this is done, the students make comparisons ('That's different, EEC passport holders are allowed more.' etc.). Then the class can be split in half (EEC and non-EEC passports), and a student appointed as customs officer in each half. The students decide what goods they are carrying, and each in turn asks the customs officer if they have to pay anything. The customs officer tells them, referring to the list when necessary.

Word Puzzle

Be careful: this is a TOP SECRET word puzzle!

1	2	3	4	5	6	7	8	1

If you answer the questions below, you'll find out which letters correspond to the numbers above – and you'll be able to fill in the word.

Strogonov had two of these.

3	7	2	2	3	5	–	–	2

What sort of papers did he have?

2	1	–	–	1	–

One of the brushes Strogonov offered to the customs officer was a . . . . . . (Be careful!)

3	7	4	6	–	–	–	–	2	–

Here is a final clue: No. 8 is the *middle* letter of the spy's *surname*.

When you have filled in the word in the top box, say what it means.

Solution: The answers to the clues are: PASSPORTS, SECRET, and PAINTBRUSH (*Not* TOOTHBRUSH, because the Number 3 must correspond to the letter P). The middle letter of 'Strogonov' is G. Therefore, the letters and numbers correspond as follows: 1–E, 2–S, 3–P, 4–I, 5–O, 6–N, 7–A, 8–G. The word produced is 'espionage', Strogonov's occupation.

Communicating

1 *Clearing up Misunderstandings*

Listen again to the beginning of Part III of the sketch, where the customs officer asked: 'Have you got anything to declare?' When Strogonov misunderstood him, he explained. Practise that section of the sketch in pairs.

Then continue these dialogues:

A Have you seen my glasses anywhere?
B Yes.
A Where?
B You were wearing them yesterday.
. . . .

A Have you been to this country before?
B Yes.
A When?
B Yesterday.
. . . .

You can use these phrases to clear up the misunderstandings:

No, you don't understand. No, what I meant was . . . I don't think you quite understand. That's not what I meant.

2 *Showing Disbelief*

Listen again to the way the customs officer showed that he did not believe the details in Strogonov's passport ('You say you're British' etc.). Listen to the tone of his voice.
Then look at the details below. A man is speaking to you on the telephone, and at the same time you are telling a friend what the man says about himself.

Name : Albert Pickles
Occupation: Minister of Defence
Address : Buckingham Palace
Salary : £100,000 per year.

Begin: 'He *says* . . .'

Exercise 1: Discuss with the class what the misunderstanding is in the first dialogue, and then ask them to use one of the phrases from the box and add to it an explanation (e.g. 'No, what I meant was: Have you seen them recently? Do you know where they are? I can't find them.') After a few examples like this, let the students practise both dialogues in pairs or groups.
Exercise 2: The students can also write similar details, and practise in threes: one 'telephoning', one receiving the phone-call and relaying the information to the third.

In Your Own Words

Re-enact the sketch in your own words, without reading from the text. Do it in short sections. These words will remind you:

For re-enacting this sketch, a table can represent the counter in the customs hall. If it is being mounted as a performance, rather than as a simple group activity in the classroom, the props involved are: peaked cap and jacket for the customs officer; mackintosh, hat and dark glasses for the spy; bottle, case, papers, clock, 'dynamite' (e.g. cardboard rolls), 'passports' (e.g. small notebooks).

* Further Role-playing Activities

Showing Disbelief

1 Give the students the following information, in order to create a situation in which they have to explain the suspicious circumstances in which they find themselves.
'A policeman finds you with the following items in your suitcase: a black mask, a set of keys, a torch, some tools and a pair of gloves. Explain why you are carrying them.'
In groups, one student can explain, and the others express their disbelief, as the customs officer did with the spy.

2 Divide the class into two groups, and tell them to work out dialogues for the following consecutive situations:
(a) A policeman finds a man standing outside a jeweller's shop late at night. He asks the man what he is doing, and responds to his story in the same way as the customs officer did to the spy's story ('I don't believe a word of it', etc.).
(b) At the police station, the policeman tells the story to the sergeant, after bringing the man in. He shows his disbelief by saying, for example: 'He *says* he was waiting for a friend.' The sergeant reacts to the story.
After the preparation stage, take a man and a policeman from one group, and let them act out their dialogue, continuing it at the police station with a sergeant from the other group.

Pronunciation Practice

1 Polite Disbelief

The customs officer believes very little of what Strogonov tells him. Play the first part of the sketch again, and let the students practise the customs officer's intonation, particularly when he says 'I see.'

2 Refusals

Re-play the section of the sketch where Strogonov offers the customs officer the brushes. Point out the different strengths with which he says 'No! . . . No! . . . No!!'.
Then, in pairs, the students should think of things to offer each other, and the 'offerer' should *insist* that the other person accept. Here are some examples:

Would you like a whisky? →	No, thank you.
How about a banana sandwich? ← →	I'd rather not, if you don't mind.
Go on. ← →	No, really, I don't want one.
Of course you do – give it a try. ← →	No! How many more times!

Explain to the students the difference between the polite forms of refusal and the more abrupt forms.

Writing

Filling in a Form

You have to write down the following information about a visitor to your country:

Name	....
Nationality	....
Date of birth	....
Date of arrival	....
Length of stay	....
Probable date of departure	....
Passport Number	....

Work in pairs, one student asking the questions and the other filling in the form.

Before starting the activity in pairs, practise the possible question forms with the students ('What is your date of birth?' or 'When were you born?'; 'How long will you be staying?' or 'How long are you going to stay?' etc.). You may like to make duplicated copies of the form, instead of allowing the students to write in their books. When the students have finished their notes, these can be used for practice in Reported Speech: the 'official' can explain what the 'visitor' told him, or the 'visitor' can explain what the 'official' asked him.

What Do You Think?

Passports

Passports are a problem. They are easy to lose, and when they expire, you have to queue to get a new one. Often the photograph doesn't look like you. It would be better if we didn't have them. Do you agree?

*For this discussion, the class could be split into groups. Some groups should work out a list of objections to passports, other groups should work out a list of reasons for having passports. Then a spokesman from a 'for' group can give some of the reasons for having passports, and a spokesman from an 'against' group can counter them. This can then develop into a general discussion.

6

The Dentist

The idea for *The Dentist* came from a member of the ETT who had studied to be a dentist. It was first performed in July 1975. On the stage it is a very visual sketch, so we have re-written it somewhat for this book. *The Dentist* has been a universally successful sketch, popular with all ages and especially well-liked in schools. It has been televised in Holland, Portugal and Yugoslavia.
This sketch is suitable for Intermediate students and above.

Attitudes and Functions

Nervousness
Is he good?
This is my first visit, you know.

Lack of Interest
Oh really?
I see.

Shock/Surprise
String? To take out a tooth?
The thirteenth floor?

Apologizing
Sorry I'm late.

Wishes
I'd like an anaesthetic.
I don't want the hammer! I want an injection.

Structure and Usage

Main Point
The use of the Present Perfect with 'the first time'.
e.g. It's the first time I've given an anaesthetic.
This is the first time I've taken out a molar.
It's the first time I've been here.

Other Points
The Present Perfect with 'before'.
e.g. I haven't seen him before.
Have you done that before?
'Want someone to . . .'
e.g. I want you to take out my tooth . . .
So you don't want me to take out that molar?

Note the Following Words and Expressions

molar anaesthetic superstitious injection It works!
How does it work? Perhaps I won't wait.

Suggested Preliminary Practice

Prepare a set of flashcards of unusual scenes, people or objects. The students can react to them, using the pattern 'It's the first time I've seen . . .'. Here are some examples:

It's the first time I've seen	a horse wearing a hat. a monkey playing the violin. a car with six wheels. a pen as big as that. someone doing that.

Even if the structure has been taught previously, it is still worth doing a short practice before listening to the sketch, as mistakes with this use of the Present Perfect are common.
You can also introduce the sketch by talking about the atmosphere in a dentist's waiting-room.

Preliminary Questions

1 How many patients were there in the waiting-room?
2 What was in the bag?
3 Why did the man and the woman leave?

6
The Dentist

SCENE	A dentist's waiting-room
CHARACTERS	Two patients: a man and a woman A 'dentist' The real dentist

The man and the woman are sitting in the waiting-room. The woman is calm, but the man is very nervous.

1 MAN — Um . . . is he good?

WOMAN — Pardon?

MAN — The dentist. Is he good?

WOMAN — I don't know.

MAN You don't know?

WOMAN No. I haven't seen him before. He's new.

MAN New!?

WOMAN Yes. It's his first day.

MAN Oh. . . . This is *my* first visit, you know.

WOMAN Oh really?

MAN It's the first time I've been here.

WOMAN Oh.

MAN Don't you understand? It's the first time I've been to the dentist in my life!

WOMAN I see.

The man looks at his watch.

MAN He's late, isn't he?

WOMAN Well, it *is* his first day.

MAN Oh well, perhaps I won't wait. I can come back tomorrow . . . or the next day.

They hear the dentist coming.

WOMAN Ah, here he comes now.

MAN (*Disappointed:*) Oh, good.

II *The 'dentist' comes in, carrying a large bag.*

'DENTIST' Ah, good morning, good morning, good morning. Sorry I'm late. Now, who's first?

WOMAN He was here first.

MAN Oh no, after you.

WOMAN No, no, you were before me.

MAN No, no, ladies first.

'DENTIST' Now, now, what seems to be the matter?

MAN I've got a bad tooth.

WOMAN So have I.

'DENTIST' Well, I can do you both at the same time.

MAN }
WOMAN } Both at the same time?

'DENTIST' Yes. I've got two pieces of string. Look!

WOMAN String? To take out a tooth? Have you done that before?

'DENTIST' Not on people, no. But I tried it this morning on the cat.

WOMAN And was the cat all right?

'DENTIST' Oh, yes! It got up, ran across the room, and jumped out of the window. And we live on the thirteenth floor.

WOMAN The thirteenth floor?

'DENTIST' Don't worry, the cat's not superstitious.

MAN But dentists don't use *string* to take out teeth!

'DENTIST' Don't they? What do you want, then?

MAN Well, to begin with, I'd like an anaesthetic.

'DENTIST' Oh, you'd like an anaesthetic, would you? Just a minute.

He takes a hammer out of his bag.

Ah, yes. Here we are.

WOMAN What's that?

'DENTIST' A hammer.

MAN Is that the anaesthetic?

'DENTIST' I'm not sure. It's the first time I've given an anaesthetic. Sit still.

He hits the man on the head, knocking him out.

MAN Ow! Ohh!

'DENTIST' Oh, it works!

He puts the hammer down.

III Now, madam, what's the matter with you?

WOMAN I've got a pain.

'DENTIST' Where?

WOMAN In my mouth.

'DENTIST' Yes, I know it's in your mouth, but which tooth?

WOMAN This one here.

'DENTIST' Ah yes, a molar.

WOMAN What are you going to do?

'DENTIST' I'm going to take it out.

WOMAN How?

'DENTIST' I don't know.

WOMAN You don't know?

'DENTIST' No. This is the first time I've taken out a molar. In fact, it's the first time I've taken out a tooth.

WOMAN The first time you've taken out a tooth!

'DENTIST' Yes. This is a very important day for me – my first extraction. Now, where's that hammer?

WOMAN Listen, I don't want the hammer and I don't want the string. I want you to take out my tooth with a pair of –

'DENTIST' A pair of scissors?

WOMAN No.

'DENTIST' A pair of socks?

WOMAN No.

'DENTIST' A pair of trousers?

WOMAN No.

'DENTIST' Oh. Just a minute.

He looks inside his bag, and takes out a large pair of forceps.

These?

WOMAN Yes, I suppose so.

'DENTIST' Right then. Open your mouth.

WOMAN But what about the anaesthetic?

'DENTIST' Oh yes. Pass me the hammer.

WOMAN I don't *want* the hammer! I want a *proper* anaesthetic. I want an injection.

'DENTIST' An injection?

WOMAN Yes.

'DENTIST' Just a minute.

He looks inside his bag again, and takes out a large syringe.

Ah yes, this is for injections, isn't it? How does it work?

WOMAN Well, you're the dentist. Don't *you* know?

'DENTIST' No. It's the first time I've used one of these. Oh well, I'll have a try. Open your mouth.

WOMAN Er, no . . . I don't think you really know . . . er . . . no, no, I'll come back another day. I –

IV *The man wakes up.*

MAN Where am I? Hey, what are you doing?

'DENTIST' I'll be with you in a moment, sir. Now, just sit still, madam . . .

MAN No, stop that! You're absolutely crazy!

WOMAN I agree. He's absolutely crazy, completely mad. Let's get out of here.

MAN Oh yes, good idea.

'DENTIST' So you don't want me to take out that molar?

WOMAN Certainly not. (*To the man:*) Come on.

MAN Yes. Good idea.

The man and the woman leave.

'DENTIST' Hmm, that worked very well.

He puts his things into the bag, laughing to himself.

'But dentists don't use *string* to take out teeth!. – 'Oh, you'd like an anaesthetic, would you?'

The real dentist arrives.

DENTIST Oh, good morning. Sorry I'm late. It's my first day. It's the first time I've been here. Are you the only one?

'DENTIST' Yes, there's just me.

DENTIST Right. You can come straight in, then.

'DENTIST' Oh, good. I hate having to wait.

Listening Comprehension

Questions

I 1 What was the difference between the two patients?
2 Did the man visit the dentist regularly?
3 How did the man feel when the 'dentist' arrived?
II 4 Why did the 'dentist' say he could do both patients at the same time?
5 What did he use for an anaesthetic?
6 Did it work?
III 7 How many molars had the 'dentist' taken out?
8 Did the woman want an anaesthetic?
IV 9 What did the man see when he woke up?
10 Why was the real dentist late?

Question 1 may lead to disagreements, as by the end of the sketch both patients are equally frightened; this is fine, as long as the students justify their answers by referring to what the patients said or how they spoke. There are two answers to Question 5: 'a hammer' or referring to Section III as well, 'a hammer and an injection'. Question 10 elicits the *Past* Perfect after 'the first time' ('It was the first time he'd been there.'): this is a useful and logical extension of the Present Perfect use. If your class has never practised the Past Perfect they can simply quote the dentist's words.

Reading Comprehension

Wrong!

Correct the following statements.

1 The 'dentist' wanted to take out two teeth with one piece of string.
2 He had already done it before, with a different patient.
3 The 'dentist' lived in a very small house.
4 He had some very up-to-date equipment.
5 There were three patients in the waiting room when the real dentist arrived.

The students should correct the statements by referring to the sketch, either in their own words or by quoting the words of the character; for example, Question 1 – 'No, he didn't. He had two pieces of string, one for each tooth.' or 'No, he didn't. He said, "I've got two pieces of string".' Question 2 will probably provoke some discussion: Is the cat a 'patient'?

Word Puzzle

One word in each of the lines below is spelt wrongly. Put the letters in the correct order, and then write the word in the correct box. This will produce a word in the vertical box. Who does the word describe?

– The *stendit.* Is he good?
– I've got a *nipa* . . . in my mouth.
– And was the *tac* all right?
– I don't want the *hermam*!
– This is the first time I've taken out a *larom*.
– A pair of *scrossis*?

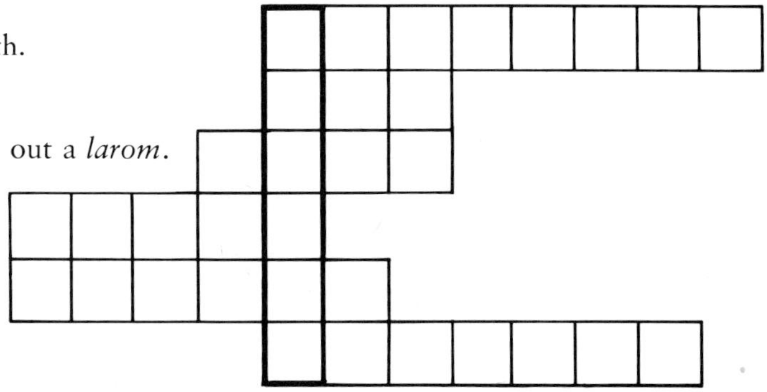

Solution: The words are: scissors/cat/pain/molar/hammer/dentist. This produces the word 'scared' in the box, which describes the man and the woman.

Communicating

1 Talking to Strangers
Listen to the first part of the sketch again. The man tries several times to start the conversation.
How would you start a conversation with someone, for example in a train compartment? Use the following expressions if they help. (Remember: If you start the conversation, you must have something to say when the stranger replies! e.g. You want a light or you want to open a window.)

Excuse me.	→ Yes?
I'm sorry to trouble you.	→ That's all right.

2 Making Excuses to Leave
Use these phrases to make apologies for leaving, adding a reason.

I'm sorry,	I can't stay.	I'm late for . . . .
I'm awfully sorry,	I have to go.	I've got to . . . .
	I must be going.	
	I must be on my way.	
	I must be getting along.	

Exercise 1: Play the first part of the sketch, and ask the students to indicate the moments when the man tries to start and re-start the conversation. Then let the students practise in pairs, as if they were strangers in a train compartment, attracting the attention of their partner and beginning a conversation. Suggest that the students continue the conversation by talking about the weather, the countryside, the time the train arrives, etc. They could then practise in threes or fours, with a third and fourth person joining in the conversation once it has started.

Exercise 2: Ask the students to suggest the reasons they might give for having to leave a party or a meeting, and then to practise combining their reasons with the phrases given.
e.g. I'm sorry I can't stay. I'm late for an appointment.
I'm sorry I must be going. I've got to catch a train.

In Your Own Words

Re-enact the sketch in your own words, without reading from the text. Do it in short sections. These words will remind you:

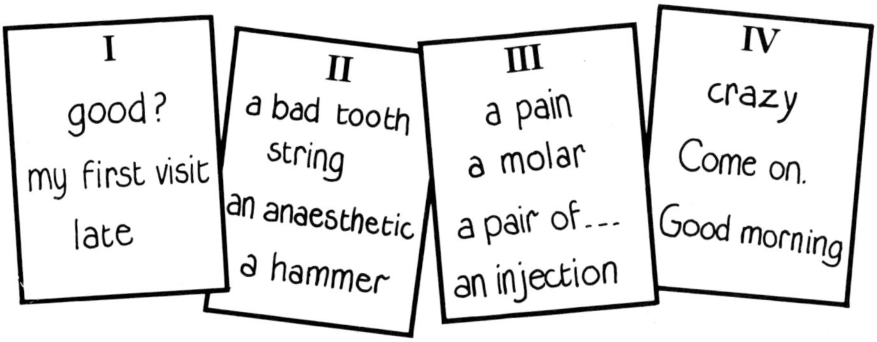

If it is possible, for re-enacting this sketch in groups in the classroom, put a few newspapers on a table or desk in front of the chairs used by the man and woman – this will suggest a waiting-room, and the two patients can hold them and flip through them during Part I. A bag of some sort is useful for the 'dentist'. For a slightly more elaborate 'performance', you will also need some pieces of string, a hammer, forceps, and a syringe (these last three perhaps made of cardboard); a white coat for the real dentist; and scissors, socks and trousers inside the 'dentist's' bag.

* Further Role-playing Activities

Refusals

These activities give the students the chance to try handling someone like the dentist in the sketch, someone who *insists* on something.

The students should improvise dialogues in these situations:

1 *Patient and doctor*
The patient has a pain in his head, but the doctor insists on examining his foot.

2 *Shopkeeper and customer*
The customer only wants a box of matches, but the shopkeeper wants to sell him something enormous and expensive.

3 *The Prime Minister and a person in the street*
The person insists on taking the Prime Minister home for a cup of tea.

Cue-cards would be useful for this activity. For example, the card given to the 'customer' could read:

You are a customer in a shop. You only want a box of matches. Do not buy anything else.

and the card given to the 'shopkeeper' could read:

You are a shopkeeper. Try to sell the customer something big and expensive. If the customer says 'No', insist.

After initial polite refusals, the 'patient', 'customer' and 'P.M.' should refuse emphatically, like this:

Look, I don't *want*	you to look at my foot! a (giant teddy bear)! a cup of tea!

Pronunciation Practice

1 Astonishment

Play the tape to the students again, and tell them to write down all the words that indicate astonishment. For example: 'New!?' 'Both at the same time?' 'String? To take out a tooth?' etc.
Then play the appropriate lines again, for the students to practise the intonation.

2 Disappointment

Play again the lines where the 'dentist' is heard arriving, and point out the way the man says 'Oh, good.' Elicit from the students the fact that he really means the opposite, and is actually disappointed that the dentist is arriving.
Tell the students that the words 'Wonderful' and 'Marvellous' can also be used in this way.
Then use the following examples and let the students respond:

I'm afraid I've lost your bicycle.
We'll have to wait another hour for the train.
I think I left your keys on the bus.
It was *your* watch that fell in the river.
I can't pay you back until next month.

Then let the students provide more examples.

Writing

A Letter to a Friend

The male patient in the sketch wrote a letter to a friend the following week. What do you think he wrote? Use the words below as a guide, and write his letter.

Dear Sheila,
tell you/something/last week. pain/tooth/went/dentist. very nervous. lady/waiting-room/I arrived. I asked/dentist/good/didn't know. more nervous!
The dentist arrived. wanted/take out/piece of string! knock out/hammer! completely mad. lady/I/managed/escape.
leaving/passed/another dentist/stairs.
Yours,
Jack.
P.S. still/pain/tooth.

The class could discuss these notes as a whole or in groups before writing the letter. Here is a possible version (several variations of detail are possible): Dear Sheila, I must tell you about something that happened to me last week. I had a pain in my tooth, so I went to the dentist. I was feeling very nervous. There was a lady in the waiting-room when I arrived. I asked her if the dentist was good, but she didn't know. That made me more nervous! The dentist arrived. He wanted to take out my tooth with a piece of string! Then he knocked me out with a hammer! He was completely mad. Fortunately, the lady and I managed to escape. As we were leaving, we passed another dentist on the stairs. Yours, Jack.
P.S. I've still got the pain in my tooth.
Notice that the notes are arranged in paragraphs, to help the students to lay out their letter.

What Do You Think?

Nervousness

Which of the following makes you most nervous?
– a visit to the dentist
– flying
– high places
– horror films
– large crowds
Why?

The students can discuss in groups. Individuals should choose the thing which makes them most nervous, tell the other members in their group why, and add any anecdotes they have about their own experiences. They can also, of course, choose to talk about a situation not on the list, if it relates more closely to their personal experience.

7

Mr Williams and the Postman

This sketch was based on a classroom activity: a revision and role-playing activity with a class of intermediate students, whose common mistake was to omit the word 'one' in expressions such as 'the red one' or 'the Japanese one'. The sketch itself was first performed in July 1976, and has been televised in Holland. In the stage-version, the ending is slightly different: Mrs Williams wins a weekend in Brighton with the postman.

This sketch is suitable for Intermediate students and above.

Attitudes and Functions

Making Sure

Mr *H.* Williams?

Mr *Henry* Williams of 65, Shakespeare Avenue?

Surprise

No?

Then why did you wake me up?

But those letters aren't for me.

Sympathy

And you, Mr Williams, you never get any letters, do you?

Choosing

Which one would you like?

– I'll have the red one, please.

Irritation

This is ridiculous.

This is very silly.

Stop wasting our time.

Structure and Usage

Main Point

Use of '. . . one'

e.g. Which one?

The red one, the white one, or the blue one?

Other Points

Present Perfect tense

e.g. You've won the red envelope!

You haven't brought any for me.

Anything/Nothing

e.g. Have you got anything for me?

There's nothing in it.

– No, there's never anything in the red one.

Note the Following Words and Expressions

service exciting ridiculous correct star prize concentrate How long will it take for . . .? What's going on? Stop wasting our time.

Note: 'The Post Office', as used in the sketch, means the organization responsible for postal services, *not* one particular post office in the street.

Suggested Preliminary Practice

The use of 'Which one?'/'the . . . one' can be practised in either of the following ways:

A Show the students two hats, two jackets and two bags (or pictures of these objects), one of each pair being suitable for a postman. Then ask questions about each pair, for example: 'One of these belongs to a postman. Which one? The white one or the grey one?' The students' answers, as they choose the suitable object, will include 'the . . . one'. (This exercise is a version of the activity which introduces the sketch in the stage-show.) You could also use clothes and objects associated with other professions.

B Ask all the students to put their watches or pens on a table. One student then picks up two items, and asks: 'Who do these belong to?' When the two owners come forward to claim them, the first student asks, for example: 'Which one is yours? The Swiss one or the Japanese one?'

Preliminary Questions

1 Why did the postman wake Mr Williams up?
2 What questions did the postman ask Mr Williams?
3 Did Mr Williams answer all the questions?

7

Mr Williams and the Postman

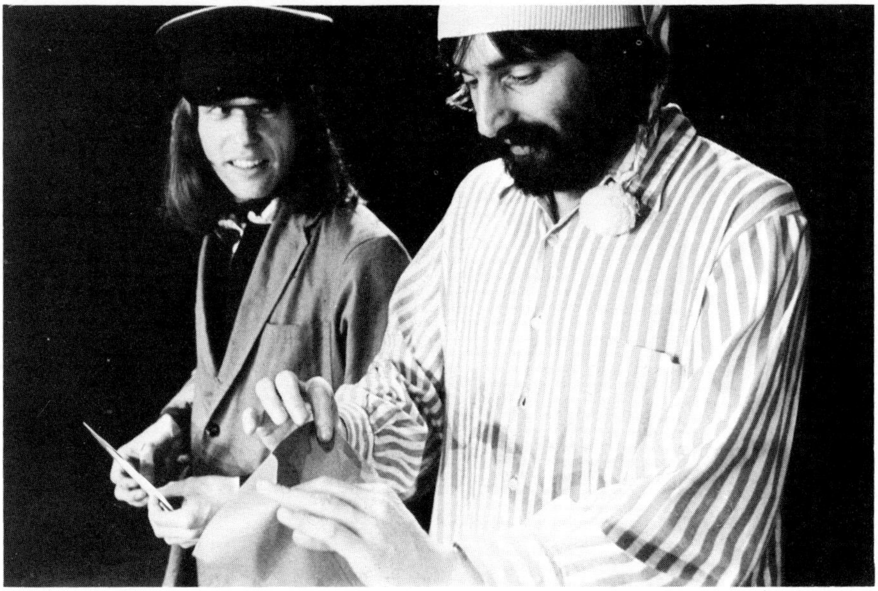

SCENE	The front door of 65, Shakespeare Avenue Early one morning
CHARACTERS	A postman Mr Henry Williams [Mr W] Mrs Agnes Williams [Mrs W]

I *The postman walks up to the front door. He knocks at the door and rings the bell.*

POSTMAN Good morning! Hello! Wake up!

Mr Williams opens the door.

Ah, good morning!

MR W Good morning.

POSTMAN Mr Williams?

MR W Yes.

POSTMAN Mr *H.* Williams?

MR W That's right.

POSTMAN Mr *Henry* Williams of 65, Shakespeare Avenue?

MR W Sixty-five? Er . . . yes. Have you got anything for me?

POSTMAN No.

MR W No?

POSTMAN No.

MR W Then why did you wake me up?

POSTMAN It's part of my job

MR W What? Waking people up?

POSTMAN Yes. It's a new service from the Post Office.

MR W Hmm. Listen – you're a postman.

POSTMAN Yes.

MR W And postmen bring letters.

POSTMAN Yes.

MR W But you haven't brought any for me.

POSTMAN Wait a minute, Mr Williams. I'm sure I can find something for you. Um . . .

He takes three letters out of his bag.

Yes, here we are. Three letters. Which one would you like? The red one, the white one, or the blue one?

II MR W But those letters aren't for me.

POSTMAN No, Mr Williams, but this is another new service from the Post Office – a new service for all those unhappy, unfortunate people who never get any letters.

MR W Oh.

POSTMAN And you, Mr Williams, you never get any letters, do you?

MR W No, I don't.

POSTMAN All right then, which one would you like? The red one, the white one, or the blue one?

MR W Um . . . I'll have the red one, please.

POSTMAN The red one is yours – if you can answer a simple question.

MR W A question?

POSTMAN Yes. Where does Queen Elizabeth the Second of England live?

MR W Why? Have you got a letter for her?

He laughs.

POSTMAN No, Mr Williams. That was the question. Where does Queen Elizabeth the Second of England live?

MR W Where does Queen Elizabeth live?

POSTMAN Yes.

MR W I don't know.

POSTMAN Mr Williams! It's easy! B-B-B-Buck –

MR W Oh, yes! Buckingham Hotel.

POSTMAN No, no! Palace!

MR W Palace Hotel?

POSTMAN No!

MR W I know! Buckingham Palace!

POSTMAN That's right! You've won the red envelope!

MR W Oh, thank you! This is very exciting!

Mr Williams opens the red envelope.

There's nothing in it.

POSTMAN No, there's never anything in the red one.

III MR W This is ridiculous!

POSTMAN No, it isn't. There are still two more envelopes.

MR W Yes, but is there anything in them?

POSTMAN Of course there is.

MR W All right. The blue one.

POSTMAN Very well, Mr Williams. Here is the question for the blue envelope. What is the approximate population of Great Britain?

MR W Er . . . thirty-five million.

POSTMAN No. Higher.

MR W Eighty-five million?

POSTMAN No. Lower.

MR W Fifty-five million people!

POSTMAN – is the correct answer! You've won the white envelope!

MR W I don't want the white one. I want the *blue* one.

POSTMAN Oh, go on. Take the white one.

MR W I don't *want* the white one.

POSTMAN Oh, all right. Here's the blue one.

MR W Thank you.

Mr Williams opens the blue envelope.

Hmm. Just a piece of paper.

POSTMAN What does it say?

MR W It says: 'You should have taken the white one.'

POSTMAN I told you.

MR W This is very silly. I'm going back to bed.

IV POSTMAN Wait a minute, Mr Williams. Today's *star prize* is in the white envelope.

MR W The star prize?

POSTMAN Yes.

MR W All right then, ask me the question.

POSTMAN Now listen carefully. If a man walks at five miles an hour, in the same direction as a car which is travelling at thirty miles an hour, how long will it take for the car to be 107 miles from the man?

MR W Eh?

POSTMAN Mr Williams! Concentrate! If a man walks at five miles an hour, in the same direction as a car which is travelling at thirty miles an hour, how long will it take for the car to be 107 miles from the man?

MR W I don't know. Three days?

POSTMAN No, no, Mr Williams. Look, why don't you ask your wife to help you?

MR W All right. Agnes!

MRS W Yes?

MR W Come here!

MRS W All right. I'm coming.

Mrs Williams comes to the door.

POSTMAN Ah, good morning, Mrs Williams.

MRS W What's going on?

MR W I'm trying to win the white one, Agnes.

MRS W The white what?

MR W The white envelope. I've already won the red one and the blue one.

MRS W Henry, what *are* you talking about?

MR W It's a competition. We answer questions and win prizes – and the star prize is in the white envelope.

POSTMAN And here is the question for the white envelope. If a man walks at five miles an hour, in the same direction as a car which is travelling at thirty miles an hour, how long will it take for the car to be 107 miles from the man?

MRS W That's easy. Four hours, sixteen minutes and forty-eight seconds.

POSTMAN Four hours, sixteen minutes and forty-eight seconds is the correct answer! You have won today's star prize. Here you are.

MRS W Ooh, thank you!

MR W Well done, Agnes.

V *Mrs Williams opens the white envelope.*

What is it?

MRS W It's just a piece of paper.

POSTMAN No, it isn't.

MR W Yes, it is. Look! Just another piece of paper!

They give the postman back the envelope and paper.

POSTMAN But, Mr Williams . . . Mrs Williams . . .

MR W Stop wasting our time. Come on, Agnes, let's go back to bed.

POSTMAN But come back! I can explain!

Mr and Mrs Williams go back into the house.

I'm sure it's not just another piece of paper. There's always a prize in the white one. Let's have a look . . . It's a cheque . . . for £500! Mr Williams! Mrs Williams!

MR W Go away!

POSTMAN But Mr Williams, you've won the star prize!

MR W Go away!!

POSTMAN Oh. . . . Well, if Mr Williams doesn't want the £500, I think I'll keep it. . . . It's a lovely day today . . .

He walks away, singing to himself.

Listening Comprehension

Questions

I 1 What time of day was it?
2 What was Mr Williams wearing?
II 3 What were the two new services from the Post Office?
4 Which envelope did Mr Williams ask for first?
5 Why was he annoyed when he got it?
III 6 Which envelope did he want next?
7 When he answered the second question correctly, what did the postman offer him?
IV 8 Was the third question easier than the others?
9 Why did Mr Williams call his wife?
10 Did Mrs Williams answer the question quickly or slowly?
V 11 Why didn't Mr and Mrs Williams take the star prize?
12 What was the star prize?

It is not explicitly stated in the sketch that Mr Williams was wearing pyjamas (dressing-gown, etc.), but in giving their answer to Question 2, the students should be able to suggest this, and should give their reasons for thinking it, i.e. Mr Williams asked the postman 'Why did you wake me up?' and said to Mrs Williams 'Let's go back to bed.' As usual, even with questions which can be answered in one word, the students should be encouraged to expand their answers by reference to the sketch; for example, the one word 'Quickly' will answer Question 10, but this can be expanded with: 'She said "That's easy" and gave the answer immediately.'

Reading Comprehension

True or False?

These statements are all about the sketch. Are they *true* or *false*?

1 The postman gave Mr Williams three letters.
2 When Mr Williams asked for the red envelope, he knew that he had to answer a question.
3 The red envelope is always empty.
4 The star prize was in the white envelope.
5 Mr and Mrs Williams could not answer the third question.
6 Mr Williams was delighted with the star prize.

Some of the statements may provoke discussion: No. 1 is not *really* true, because there were no *letters* in the envelopes, although the postman did refer to them as 'letters' at the end of Section I; No. 5 is partially true, because *Mr* Williams could not answer the question; in commenting on No. 6, it is important to point out that Mr Williams did not wait to find out what the star prize was. – If he had done so, he would have been delighted. The other three are more straightforward: No. 2 is definitely false, and Nos. 3 and 4 are definitely true.

Word Puzzle

Fill in the words in the horizontal boxes. The letters in the vertical box will then spell a word: a quick way of sending letters.

1 The Queen of England lives in one.

2 Waking people up is a new . . . . from the Post Office.

3 The colour of the first envelope.

4 The answer to the second question was: Fifty-five . . . . people.

5, 6 The . . . . was in the white envelope.

7 The postman didn't bring any for Mr Williams!

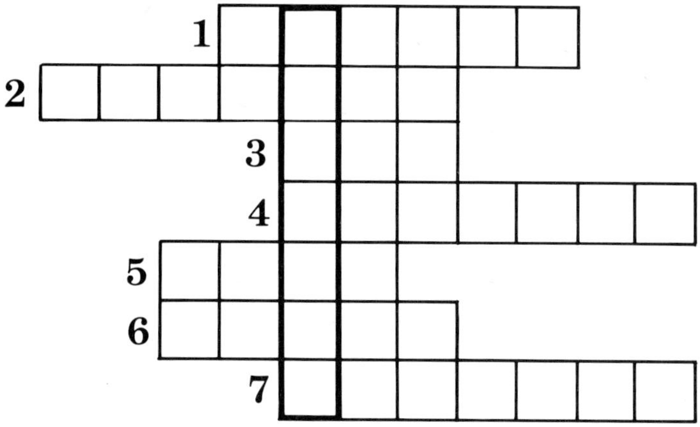

Solution: 1 palace 2 service 3 red 4 million 5 star 6 prize 7 letters The word in the vertical box is therefore 'Airmail'.

Communicating

Making Sure

A Listen to the first part of the sketch again. The postman is making sure of Mr Williams' exact name and address. Practise the six lines from 'Good morning.' to ' . . . 65, Shakespeare Avenue?'
Then practise similar dialogues in pairs. Use your own names and addresses, or give yourselves English names and addresses.

B Practise making sure of other facts and figures. First this dialogue at a railway station:

Is this Platform 4?	→ Yes.
And is this the 9.55?	→ I think so.
The 9.55 to Edinburgh?	→ Yes, I think it is.
Does it stop at Newcastle?	→ I expect so.
Thank you.	→ Not at all.

Then invent a similar dialogue in the queue at a cinema.

Exercise A: When the students listen to the lines from the sketch again, point out the way the postman stresses the important words, the words he is checking ('Mr *H.* Williams?' 'Mr *Henry* Williams?' '*65* . . .'). When practising the similar dialogues in pairs, the students can write their own or their invented names and addresses on pieces of paper, and exchange them with their partners. They can then use these pieces of paper as if they were envelopes which they are delivering, and 'make sure' of the names and addresses by referring to them.
Exercise B: Before the students invent their own dialogues in pairs, it may be useful for them to suggest the kinds of questions they might ask in the situations given. For example, in the cinema queue, whether they are in the right queue for a particular film, what time the film starts, how much the seats are, etc. They can then practise in pairs, making some of their questions genuine enquiries ('How much are the tickets?') and some questions for confirmation ('It starts at nine o'clock, doesn't it?').

In Your Own Words

Re-enact the sketch in your own words, without reading from the text. Do it in short sections. These words will remind you:

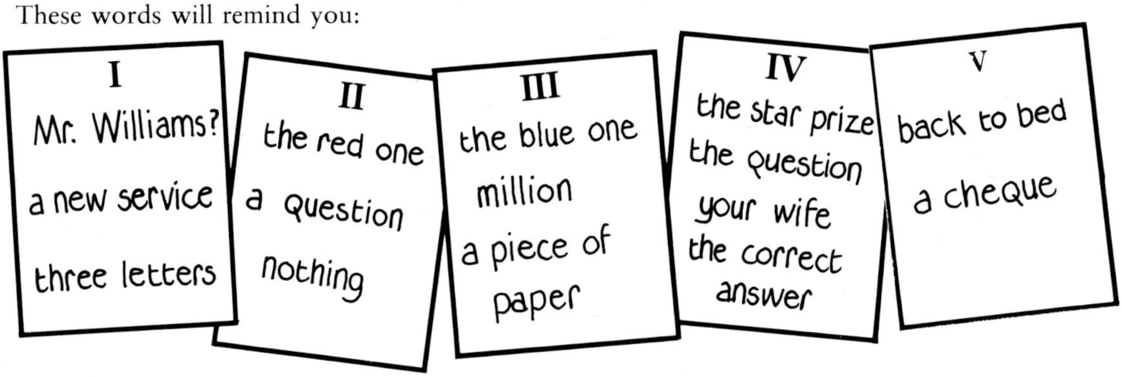

All that is really needed for re-enacting this sketch in class is three envelopes, two of which have pieces of paper inside (one to represent the note, and one the cheque) and one of which is empty. Alternatively, folded pieces of paper, coloured if possible, can be used to represent the envelopes. A handy extra 'prop' is a bag for the postman, any kind of bag will do, simply to make him feel more like a postman. For a more elaborate 'performance', costumes for the characters will be needed – hat, jacket and bag for the postman, dressing-gowns and slippers, etc. for Mr and Mrs Williams. Even in a simple classroom re-enactment, however the students should be encouraged to visualize the situation at Mr Williams' front door, and to mime the postman's knocking and ringing the bell, Mr Williams opening the door, attempting to close it and go back inside, finally doing so, etc.

* Further Role-playing Activities

1 An Alternative Ending

The students can improvise the dialogue that would have taken place if Mr and Mrs Williams had opened the white envelope and found the cheque for £500: firstly the dialogue with the postman, and secondly the dialogue between Mr and Mrs Williams (after the postman has gone) speculating on what they will do with the prize money.

2 Games with Puzzles

The students can act out a TV game in which prizes can be won. In groups, they should make up the questions and decide on the prizes. One group can then appoint a 'question-master' who will put the group's questions to 'contestants' from another group. All the groups take a turn in this way. In playing the game, suggest that the 'question-masters' use expressions like:

Here's the question for the first prize.
The first prize is a (bottle of milk)!
Congratulations! You've won the (bottle of milk)!
Concentrate! Listen carefully!
Today's star prize is . . . .
Go on! Try another question.

(The 'question-masters' may like to *introduce* the games using some of the expressions from the 'World Record' sketch. See Further Role-playing Activities, p. 87).
The 'tension' can be increased by making the game one of the 'all or nothing' variety, i.e. if a contestant wins five prizes, but fails to answer the sixth question correctly, he loses all his

prizes. The questions which the students invent can be either general knowledge questions or questions about *English* words, places or institutions (similar to the postman's first two questions in the sketch).

Pronunciation Practice

Stress

A Play section III of the sketch again. Draw the students' attention to the way Mr Williams says:
'I don't want the white one. I want the *blue* one.'
Practise the stress pattern.

B Give further practice with this stress pattern, by getting the students to respond to the following prompt sentences:
1 Here you are, Mr Jones – the purple shirt you ordered.
2 I think you'd like the silver watch.
3 I'm sure you'll prefer this English TV set, Mrs Smith.
4 Never mind the Japanese car, sir. This Irish one is very good.
5 A Swiss camera? Why not take this nice Australian one, sir?
Make sure that the contrasting adjective receives good clear stress.

Writing

A Letter of Complaint

Mr Williams wanted to make a complaint about the postman. He wrote a letter to the Post Office.
Below is the part of the letter where Mr Williams explained what happened. The words are in the wrong order. Write the sentences correctly.

asleep was in bed I. heard ring woke I the door-bell when I up. the door to went I. your standing was of one postmen there. me didn't told he any for letters he have me. funny it was didn't I think.

Complete Mr Williams' letter, by writing the beginning and the end.

The students can work in groups to decipher the muddled sentences, and then the class as a whole can decide on the correct version, discussing any differences between groups' versions. (The correct version reads: 'I was asleep in bed. I woke up when I heard the door-bell ring. I went to the door. One of your postmen was standing there. He told me he didn't have any letters for me. I didn't think it was funny.') Then discuss with the students how the letter might be completed; mention these sections:

1 The addresses at the top, with the date.
2 The 'salutation' ('Dear Sir,') and the first paragraph. Give them an opening expression such as: 'I wish to make a complaint about one of your postmen, and an incident which took place this morning.')
3 Mr Williams' account of what happened, beginning with the sentences which have been 'deciphered'.
4 The conclusion. Give them a closing expression such as: 'Please inform me of the action you intend to take'.

5 The 'signing-off' ('Yours faithfully,') and signature.

The letter can then be written in class or for homework, using these notes.

What Do You Think?

Prizes

Which of the following prizes would you like to win?
– A fortnight's holiday in Miami.
– A round-the-world cruise on a luxury liner.
– Free air travel for a year.
– The best stereo system in the world.
– A year's supply of food and drink.
– Dinner with your favourite film star or pop singer.
Give reasons for your choice.

The students can work in small groups. The individuals in the groups spend a few minutes deciding on their choice (and making notes on their reasons if they wish). They then explain to the other members of their group what they would choose and why. After they have explained their choices, they can try to persuade one another to change their minds, by comparing their choices. (They could also discuss any prizes they have won in real life: what they won, and how they won it.) As a conclusion to the activity, with the whole class, you could put the six prizes on the blackboard and mark alongside each one the number of students who chose it, taking a show of hands for each one, and finally invite one student for each prize to tell the class the reasons for their choice.

8

The Bank

The idea for this sketch came from an old joke about writing a cheque to cover an overdraft. We also liked the idea of a customer pretending not to understand his bank manager, and a bank robber who was not very competent, so we combined these elements and wrote this sketch. It was first performed in July 1976. Since then, it has been very popular in the stage-show, and has also been televised in Holland, Belgium and Mexico. For this book, the stage version has been slightly shortened and the ending altered. On stage, Mr Moore and the robber went off together to rob another bank, leaving the manager to sing a song.
This sketch is suitable for Intermediate students and above.

Attitudes and Functions
Explaining Clearly
I don't think you quite understand. You see, if you . . .
More, Mr Moore. M-O-R-E, *more*.

Correcting
Not *honey* – *money.*
No, no, no. The other side.

Paraphrasing
In the red. Overdrawn.
It means that . . .

Polite, Business-like Forms
Do sit down, Mr Moore. The situation is like this.
Can I help you?
I'll be with you in a moment.

Telling Someone How to do Something
You take the note, go into the bank, and . . . .

Structure and Usage
Main Point
Comparisons, using 'more/less . . . than' and 'twice/half as much as'.
e.g. You've taken more money out of the bank than you've put in.
You spend twice as much as you earn.
– Yes, I earn half as much as I spend.
Other Points
'Shall' used in offers or suggestions.
e.g. I'll write you a cheque, shall I?
'Would' used in requests.
e.g. Would you bring me some coffee?
'Would you like . . .' used in polite questions.
e.g. Would you like to sit down?

Note the Following Words and Expressions
Expressions connected with banking: in the red overdrawn account open an account cheque cheque-book
Other expressions: Nobody move! for a moment at the moment in a moment

Suggested Preliminary Practice
Practise the comparisons, by giving the students some statistics to compare. For example:

TWO AUTHORS		
	Henry Swift	Ted Milton
INCOME:	£8,000 a year	£4,000 a year
BOOKS WRITTEN:	twelve	six
COUNTRIES VISITED:	France, Spain, Italy, Germany	France, Switzerland
CHILDREN:	four	two

Put this table on the blackboard. Using the information in it, the students can make comparisons in these forms:

(a) '. . . more/less . . . than . . .'
(b) '. . . twice/half as much/many . . . as . . .'

For example: 'Henry Swift has written more books than Ted Milton', 'Ted Milton earns less money than Henry Swift', 'Henry Swift has got more children than Ted Milton', 'Ted Milton has visited half as many countries as Henry Swift' and so on.
Instead of this table, you could of course use a different one, e.g. comparing two countries, two cities, etc.
If you feel that practice of this type is not needed, introduce the sketch by presenting some of the vocabulary and expressions connected with banks. (Note, however, that it is not vital to present the expressions 'in the red' and 'overdrawn', as they are explained in the sketch itself, and part of the fun of the sketch springs from these explanations.)

Preliminary Questions
1 Why did the bank manager want to see Mr Moore?
2 Why did Mr Moore have a problem with money?
3 How did he solve his problem?

8

The Bank

SCENE	The manager's office in a bank
CHARACTERS	Miss D. Posit, the bank manager Monica, Miss Posit's secretary Mr Moore, a customer A bank robber

I

	Miss Posit is sitting at her desk. The intercom buzzes.
MISS POSIT	Yes, Monica?
MONICA	Miss Posit, there's a gentleman to see you. Mr Moore.
MISS POSIT	Ah, yes. Mr Moore. Bring him in please, Monica.
MONICA	Yes, Miss Posit.
	Monica brings Mr Moore in.
	Mr Moore.
MISS POSIT	Good morning, Mr Moore.
MR MOORE	Good morning.
MISS POSIT	Thank you, Monica.
	Monica leaves the office.
	Do sit down, Mr Moore.
MR MOORE	Thank you.
	He sits down.
MISS POSIT	Now, Mr Moore, the situation is like this. Your account is in the red.
MR MOORE	Pardon?
MISS POSIT	In the red.
MR MOORE	I'm sorry. I don't understand.
MISS POSIT	In the red. Overdrawn.
MR MOORE	'Overdrawn'. No, I'm sorry. I've never heard that word before in my life.

MISS POSIT It's very simple, Mr Moore. It means that you've taken more money *out* of the bank than you've put *in*.

MR MOORE Oh, I see. Thank you very much.

MISS POSIT I don't think you quite understand, Mr Moore. It means that you've put in *less* than you've taken out.

MR MOORE Oh.

MISS POSIT Your account is overdrawn. £200 overdrawn.

MR MOORE £200 overdrawn. I see. Well, don't worry. I can put that right immediately.

MISS POSIT Oh, good.

MR MOORE Yes, I'll write you a cheque, shall I?

He takes out his cheque-book and begins to write.

Now . . . two hundred pounds . . .

MISS POSIT Mr Moore, Mr Moore, if you write me a cheque for £200, you'll be overdrawn *more*, Mr Moore.

MR MOORE I beg your pardon?

MISS POSIT *More*, Mr Moore. M-O-R-E, *more*.

MR MOORE No, no . . . *double*-O . . . M-double-O-R-E, Mr *Moore*. It *is* my name.

MISS POSIT Mr Moore, I don't think you quite understand the situation. You see –

The robber comes in suddenly.

11 ROBBER Nobody move!

Miss Posit continues speaking to Mr Moore.

MISS POSIT – you see, if you write me a cheque for £200 –

ROBBER I said: 'Nobody move!'

MISS POSIT Can I help you?

ROBBER That's better. *You* –

MR MOORE Me?

ROBBER Yes. Read this.

He gives Mr Moore a note.

MR MOORE Oh. O.K. (*Reading:*) 'Two pounds of tomatoes, six eggs, and a packet of chocolate biscuits.'

ROBBER No, no, no. The other side.

MR MOORE Oh, sorry. (*Reading:*) 'Give me all your . . . honey, or I'll . . . kiss you.'

ROBBER Not *honey* – *money*.

MR MOORE Oh, sorry. (*Reading:*) 'Give me all your *money*, or I'll kiss you.'

ROBBER Not *kiss* – *kill*!

MR MOORE Oh. Er . . . Miss Posit, I think this is for you.

He gives the note to Miss Posit.

MISS POSIT (*Reading:*) 'Give me all your money, or I'll kill you.' I see. Would you sit down for a moment?

ROBBER Sit down?

MISS POSIT Yes, I'm very busy at the moment. Please sit over there.

ROBBER But –

MISS POSIT I'll be with you in a moment.

The robber sits down.

III | | Now, Mr. Moore. How much do you earn?

MR MOORE	£35 a week.
ROBBER	Excuse me –
MISS POSIT	Just one moment, *please*! . . . So you earn £35 a week. How much do you spend?
MR MOORE	£70 a week.
ROBBER	Excuse me –
MISS POSIT	One moment, *please*!! . . . £70 a week. So you spend twice as much as you earn.
MR MOORE	Yes, I earn half as much as I spend.
MISS POSIT	How do you do it?
MR MOORE	It's easy. I use my cheque-book.
MISS POSIT	Exactly, Mr Moore!
ROBBER	*Excuse me!*
MISS POSIT	Yes!!
ROBBER	*I* make £2,000 a week.
MISS POSIT	£2,000 a week? And how much do you spend?
ROBBER	£1,000 a week.
MISS POSIT	Really? So you *save* £1,000 a week.
ROBBER	Yes.
MISS POSIT	(*Very politely:*) Would you like to sit here?
ROBBER	Thank you.
MISS POSIT	Mr Moore, would you sit over there for a moment?
	The robber and Mr Moore change places.
	So you *save* £1,000 a week.
ROBBER	Yes.
MISS POSIT	Tell me . . . where do you keep this money?
ROBBER	Here. In this bag.
	He puts a large bag full of money on the desk.
MISS POSIT	Oh. Oh, yes. Very nice. Um . . . would you like to open an account, Mr . . . ?
ROBBER	Mr Steele.
MISS POSIT	Steele. I see. S-T-double-E-L-E?
ROBBER	Yes, that's right.
MISS POSIT	Well, just excuse me one moment, Mr Steele, and I'll get the necessary papers.
ROBBER	Certainly.
	Miss Posit leaves the office.

IV

MR MOORE	Excuse me . . .
ROBBER	Yes?
MR MOORE	You make £2,000 a week.
ROBBER	Yes.
MR MOORE	How do you do it?
ROBBER	I rob banks.
MR MOORE	Oh, I see. You rob banks and *steal* the money.

ROBBER Yes.

MR MOORE How do you do it?

ROBBER It's easy. You take a gun –

MR MOORE I haven't got a gun.

ROBBER Oh . . . well, borrow mine.

MR MOORE Thank you very much.

Mr Moore takes the gun and fires it.

ROBBER Be careful! . . . You take a gun and you take a note.

MR MOORE Oh yes, the note. That's very good. I like that. (*Reading:*) 'Two pounds of tomatoes, six eggs –'

ROBBER The other side!

MR MOORE Oh, yes. (*Reading:*) 'Give me all your honey, or I'll kiss you!'

ROBBER '*Money*' and '*kill*'!

MR MOORE Oh, yes.

ROBBER You take the note, go into the bank, and put the note on the bank manager's desk.

MR MOORE Is that all?

ROBBER Yes.

MR MOORE I see.

V *Miss Posit comes back into the office.*

MISS POSIT Ah, yes. Now, Mr Steele –

MR MOORE Give me all your honey . . . *money*, or I'll kiss . . . *kill* you.

MISS POSIT Money, Mr Moore? Certainly. Take this bag.

She gives Mr Moore the robber's bag.

MR MOORE Oh, thank you. That was easy.

ROBBER Yes, but –

MISS POSIT Mr Moore, your account is still £200 overdrawn.

MR MOORE Oh, yes. Well . . . um . . . Here you are.

He gives her £200 from the robber's bag.

£50 . . . £100 . . . £150 . . . £200.

ROBBER But . . . But . . .

MISS POSIT Thank you, Mr Moore.

MR MOORE Goodbye.

Mr Moore leaves.

MISS POSIT Now, Mr Steele . . . your account . . .

ROBBER But . . . But . . . But . . .

MISS POSIT Mr Steele . . .

ROBBER Just a minute! I think something's gone wrong. Hey, you! Come back! Bring back my money and my gun! Come back!

He runs after Mr Moore.

MISS POSIT (*On the intercom:*) Monica, would you bring me some coffee, please? Some *strong black* coffee . . .

Listening Comprehension

Questions

I 1 Mr Moore said 'I don't understand'. Was it true?
2 What suggestion did Mr Moore make?
II 3 What was written on the robber's note?
4 Was the manager frightened of the robber?
III 5 Did the robber and Mr Moore both have a problem with money?
6 Why did the manager suddenly speak to the robber politely?
IV 7 What did the robber explain to Mr Moore?
8 What did he give Mr Moore?
V 9 How did Mr Moore pay the manager?
10 Who was happy and who was unhappy at the end?

In answering Question 3, the students can mention *both* sides of the robber's note. In answering Question 4, they should support their answer by referring to the manager's way of speaking to the robber (she remained very businesslike and told him to sit and wait, etc.). For question 10, all three characters should be referred to: the manager and Mr Moore being pleased as the overdraft problem has been settled, and the robber annoyed and slightly confused after the loss of his money.

Reading Comprehension

A Letter and Some Instructions

Read these twelve sentences. Six are from a letter (from the bank manager to a customer) and six are from some instructions (from the robber to another robber, explaining how to rob a bank).
Decide which sentences come from the letter and which sentences come from the instructions. Then put them in the correct order.

1 You will also need a note.
2 Yours sincerely, D. Posit (Manager).
3 Go into the bank and put the note on the manager's desk.
4 The amount is £352.
5 How to rob a bank. First, you'll need a gun.
6 Dear Mr Bennett.
7 If not, the bank will refuse to renew your cheque-book.
8 The manager will read the note and give you some money.
9 You won't have to fire it, just point it at the manager.
10 I am writing to inform you that your account is overdrawn.
11 It should say: Give me all your money or I'll kill you.
12 I hope you will correct this situation as soon as possible.

The students can do this exercise individually or in pairs. They should first read all the sentences through, and then write them in two columns, one for the manager's letter, and one for the robber's instructions. They should then look at their first column and put the sentences into the right order, and do the same for their second column, thus producing the letter and instructions. There are plenty of clues to help the students deduce the correct order (pronouns and articles which refer back, words like 'also', 'first' and so on). The correct orders are: The letter: 6, 10, 4, 12, 7, 2; the instructions: 5, 9, 1, 11, 3, 8.

Word Puzzle

Fill in the correct words.

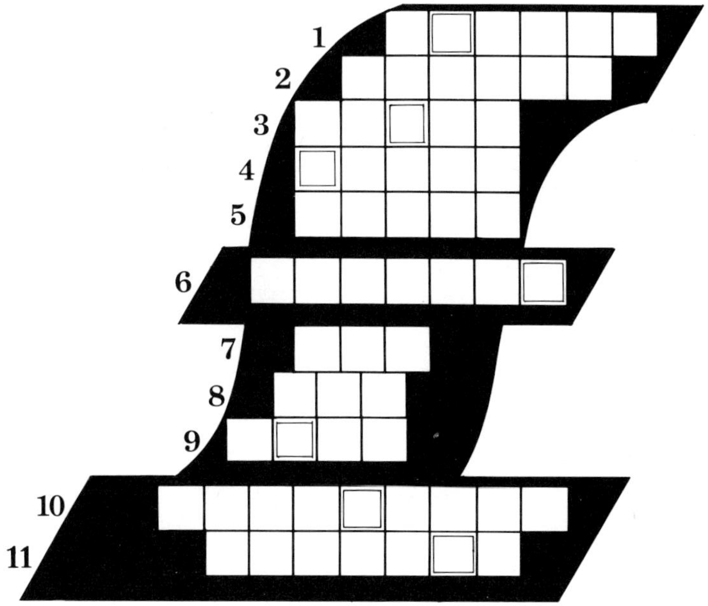

1 The bank . . . . had a gun and a note.
2 Mr Moore wanted to pay by . . . .
3 He wanted to . . . . a cheque for £200.
4 The robber's name sounded like the word '. . . . .'
5 Mr Moore . . . . twice as much as he earned.
6 His . . . . was not in the black.
7 The robber came to . . . . the bank.
8 Mr Moore's account was in the . . . .
9 Mr Steele did not really want to . . . . an account.
10 Mr Moore's account was £200 . . . .
11 The bank . . . . had a secretary called Monica.

When you have filled in all the words, take the letters in the special boxes. Arrange them into a word, one that is very similar to the manager's name.

Solution: 1 robber 2 cheque 3 write 4 steal 5 spent 6 account 7 rob 8 red 9 open 10 overdrawn 11 manager. The letters in the special boxes can be arranged to spell the word 'deposit': a *verb* meaning to put money into a bank account or a *noun* meaning the money put in (the manager's name was D. Posit).

Communicating

1 Paraphrasing

Listen again to the beginning of the sketch. Notice how the manager explained the situation to Mr Moore, particularly these lines:

Miss Posit:	Your account is *in the red*. . . .
Mr Moore:	I'm sorry. I don't understand.
Miss Posit:	In the red. Overdrawn. . . . It means that you've taken more money *out* of the bank than you've put *in*.

She first gave another word, and then explained.
Practise in pairs, making similar short dialogues. Start with these sentences:

1 This passport *has expired.*
2 This £5 note is *a forgery.*
3 This necklace is *priceless.*

2 *Telling Someone How to do Something*
Listen again to section IV of the sketch. Notice how the robber told Mr Moore how to rob a bank, using the Present Simple tense:

Mr Moore:	How do you do it?
Robber:	You take a gun . . . and you take a note. . . . You take the note, go into the bank, and put the note on the bank manager's desk.

In pairs, practise similar explanations. You can explain how to:

– make an omelette
– make a cup of tea
– send a telegram

or choose something else. Remember these phrases:

How do you do it? What do you do first? What do you do next/then? What do you do after that?	First, you . . . . Then you . . . . After that, you . . . .

* **Exercise 1:** Play the appropriate part of the sketch to the students again, and allow them to practise the relevant lines of paraphrasing. Then ask for suggestions from the class as a whole for the 'passport' example (This might run: 'I'm sorry. I don't understand.' – 'It's expired. It's finished. It means that you can't use it any more.'), and let them work out possible paraphrases for the other examples, in pairs or in groups.
Exercise 2: Play the appropriate part of the sketch again, and then let the students work in pairs, either on the activities suggested, or choosing their own (e.g. explanations of things with which they are familiar from their own interests or hobbies). After the pair-work, several students can explain to the whole class how something is done.

In Your Own Words

Re-enact the sketch in your own words, without reading from the text. Do it in short sections. These words will remind you:

For re-enacting in the classroom, use a desk for the 'manager' to sit behind, with two other chairs, one for 'Mr Moore', and one for the 'robber'. Other simple 'props' which are useful are: a small notebook or real cheque-book for Mr Moore, a bag and a piece of paper for the robber, and some papers for the manager's desk. For a more elaborate 'performance' the following are helpful: a telephone and a nameplate on the manager's desk, a gun and some bundles of money for the robber, and costumes as desired for the four characters.

* Further Role-playing Activities

1 Explaining Clearly

Give the students cue-cards based on the examples in the first 'Communicating' exercise on page 77 ('Paraphrasing'), i.e.

1 Traveller and immigration official.
2 Shopkeeper and customer.
3 Jeweller and person who has found an old necklace in their attic.

The idea is that the official, the shopkeeper and the jeweller should try to explain what they mean ('This passport has expired', 'This £5 note is a forgery', 'This necklace is priceless'), while the traveller, the customer and the 'necklace finder' should pretend for as long as possible that they do not understand, just as Mr Moore did in the sketch.
The cue-cards for No. 1, for example, might look like this:

TRAVELLER	OFFICIAL
You are a traveller. Your passport has expired. Pretend you do not understand when the official explains this to you.	You are an immigration official. You are talking to a traveller whose passport has expired. Explain this to him/her.

2 A conversation with a Bank Manager

The students can improvise conversations in pairs or threes. A customer (or two customers) visit(s) a bank manager, to try and borrow some money. The manager wants to know what the money is for, but even when he finds out is not very willing to lend it.

Pronunciation Practice

1 Increasing Insistence

Play a short section of the sketch to the students again, beginning with:

Miss Posit: (*Reading:*) 'Give me all your money . . .'

and ending with:

Robber: *I* make £2,000 a week.

Point out to the students the three times the robber says 'Excuse me', and the way in which he increases his insistence each time.
Then ask them to find three sentences by Miss Posit in the same section, in which she increases her insistence in a similar way. They should be able to identify them fairly easily as:

– Would you sit down for a moment?/I'll be with you in a moment.
– Just one moment, *please*!
– One moment, *please*!!

2 Stress to Make Contrasts Clear

Let the students hear again and imitate Miss Posit's sentence in section I of the sketch:

'It means that you've taken more money *out* of the bank than you've put *in*.'

Draw their attention to the heavy stress on the words 'out' and 'in'.
Then ask them to use similar stress to make these sentences clear:

1 This switch goes *up* for *'Off'*, and *down* for *'On'*.
2 You're supposed to jump *over* the water, not *into* it.
3 I wanted the lamp *on* the bookcase, not *in* it.

Put the sentences (and any others of your own) on the blackboard, without marking the stressed words in any way at first. When the students have worked out which words need the strong stress, and have said the sentences aloud, get them to mark the stresses by circling or underlining the appropriate words.

Writing

A List of Instructions

Choose one of the following, and write the necessary list of instructions:

(a) *A recipe*. Explain how to cook a dish. Choose one that you can do very well. Write first the *ingredients*, and then the method of making the dish (in a numbered list).
(b) *Making a telephone call*. Explain how to make a telephone call from a public telephone in your country. Write first the coins needed, and then the method of making the call (in a numbered list).

This can be done as homework, or as a group activity in class (with preparation similar to the second 'Communicating' exercise, 'Telling someone how to do something', on p. 78). In their lists of instructions, the students should use Imperatives, rather than the Present Simple tense, which is used in giving similar explanations orally.

What Do You Think?

Pay

Mr Moore earned £35 a week, and the bank robber made £2,000 a week. Some people earn much more money than others. Do you think this is right? Who should earn a lot of money? Which would you prefer: a job you enjoyed, but which was badly paid? Or a job you hated, but which was well paid?

* In groups, the students can discuss these and related questions. If individuals feel that everyone should receive the same pay, they should say why. If they feel that some people deserve more money than others, they should say which people and why. They can then discuss their own preferences for jobs, either speculating about their future, or saying why they chose their jobs if they are adults.

9
World Record

The idea for this sketch came from a role-playing activity devised by a member of the ETT to practise the Present Perfect Continuous tense with a class. The students were filmed on video and the activity was a great success. Everyone agreed that a sketch should be written for the show, based on the idea, and *World Record* was the result. It was first performed in July 1974. It later formed the basis for a programme on German TV, in the Radio Bremen series 'Speak for Yourself', where the emphasis was placed on the language used in clarifying misunderstandings; the sketch has also been televised in Holland. For this book, we have adapted the original stage-version slightly, adding reactions from TV viewers who do not appear in that version.
This sketch is suitable for Intermediate students and above.

Attitudes and Functions
Making Suggestions
Let's have a look at it.

Getting Information
What are you doing?
How long have you been standing on one leg?
What's the world record?

Clearing Up Misunderstandings
How does it feel?
– Hot!
No, no, no! How does it feel to be approaching the world record?
What's the world record?
– I'm not trying to break a world record.

Structure and Usage
Main Point
The Present Perfect Continuous tense
e.g. How long have you been leaning on that brush?
– I've been leaning on this brush for 3 hours and 17 minutes.
Note: In this sketch the Present Perfect Continuous tense is only used to describe an activity which is still in progress. The other uses are not covered here.

Other Points
The Present Continuous tense
e.g. What are you doing?
– I'm looking for my trousers.

Relative Pronouns
e.g. The programme that gives *you* the chance to break a world record.
Two people who are trying to break world records.

Note the Following Words and Expressions
a world record break a record fascinating studio contestant viewers approaching knock (someone/something) over You've got a long way to go Get out of the way
Note: The expressions 'You've got a long way to go' and '(four) minutes to go' occur several times in the sketch, and can easily be understood from the context.

Suggested Preliminary Practice
Practise the Present Perfect Continuous tense with, for example, a set of pictures showing various activities in progress, and a clock face. Firstly, establish what is happening in each picture: use questions in the Present Continuous ('What's he/she doing?' 'What are they doing?'). Then move the clock forward, for example, twenty minutes, in order to elicit sentences in the Present Perfect Continuous ('He/She's been ---ing . . . for twenty minutes.' 'They've been ---ing . . . for twenty minutes.') in answer to questions beginning 'How long . . . ?'
The students can then take over the questions as well, and can alter the clock face to provide variety in the answers.
If the students are reasonably familiar with the Present Perfect Continuous tense, you could introduce the sketch by:

(a) asking a few questions, using the tense, about the students themselves, e.g. whether they drive and how long they have been driving, etc. or:
(b) briefly talking about world records, e.g. who has run the fastest 100 metres, who has jumped the highest, and so on, particularly referring to any world record holders from their country.

Preliminary Questions
1 How many people were trying to break a world record?
2 Were they trying to break the same one?
3 What happened to Mr Hargreaves?

9

World Record

SCENE — A TV studio

CHARACTERS — Michael Moonshine
Albert Hargreaves
Mrs Hargreaves
Mabel Phillips
A man
George and Hilda, TV viewers

I GEORGE — Hilda, what's on television?

HILDA — Er . . .

She looks at a newspaper.

. . . a programme called 'Your chance to break a world record'.

GEORGE — What's that?

HILDA — (*Reading:*) 'The fascinating programme in which people try to break world records.'

GEORGE — Oh, let's have a look at it.

He switches on the television. The programme has just begun.

II MICHAEL M — Thank you, thank you, thank you. Yes, ladies and gentlemen, this is the programme that gives *you* the chance to break a world record. We have here in the studio tonight two people who are trying to break world records. Let's meet them and see what they're doing. Tell me, sir, what is your name?

ALBERT — Albert Hargreaves.

MICHAEL M — Albert Hargreaves. Well, Albert, what are you doing?

ALBERT — I'm standing on one leg in a bucket of hot soup.

MICHAEL M — Ladies and gentlemen, he's standing on one leg in a bucket of hot soup!

The audience applaud.

Albert, how long have you been standing on one leg in that bucket of hot soup?

ALBERT — I've been standing here for six hours and fifty-eight minutes.

MICHAEL M — And what is the world record for standing on one leg in a bucket of hot soup?

ALBERT — The world record is seven hours and three minutes, Michael.

MICHAEL M — Seven hours and three minutes! And you've been standing there for *six* hours and fifty-*nine* minutes now. Well, Albert, you've only got *four* more minutes to go!

The audience applaud.

Albert, you've been standing on one leg in that bucket of hot soup for almost seven hours now.

ALBERT — That's right, Michael.

MICHAEL M — Tell me – is the soup still hot?

ALBERT — Yes. My wife's been coming in every half-hour with more hot soup. Here she comes now.

Mrs Hargreaves comes in.

MRS HAR — Here you are, Albert.

She pours some hot soup into the bucket.

ALBERT — Aaargh!

MICHAEL M — Well, I'm glad it's *your* leg in the soup, Albert, and not mine.

The audience laugh.

III — Now we have another contestant in the studio, a very charming young lady. Can you tell the viewers your name?

MABEL — Mabel Phillips.

MICHAEL M — Mabel Phillips. Well, Mabel, what are *you* doing?

MABEL — I'm leaning on this brush.

MICHAEL M — She's leaning on a brush, ladies and gentlemen!

The audience applaud.

Mabel, how long have you been leaning on that brush?

MABEL — I've been leaning on this brush for three hours and seventeen minutes.

MICHAEL M — She's been leaning on the brush for three hours and seventeen minutes. What is the world record for leaning on a brush, Mabel?

MABEL — Thirty-seven hours and fifty-six minutes.

MICHAEL M — Thirty-seven hours and fifty-six minutes! And you've been leaning on that brush for three hours and seventeen minutes. Well, Mabel, you've got . . . three, four, five, six – you've got a long way to go!

The audience laugh.

IV — Well, Albert has been standing on one leg in his bucket of hot soup for *seven* hours and *one* minute, so he's only got *two* more minutes to go! Poor Mabel's got a *long* way to go. . . . And here is another young man – and he hasn't got any trousers on.

The audience laugh.

Now, sir, what are *you* doing?

MAN I'm looking for my trousers.

MICHAEL M I can see that. And how *long* have you been looking for your trousers?

MAN I've been looking for my trousers for five minutes.

MICHAEL M And what's the world record?

MAN Pardon?

MICHAEL M What's the world record for looking for trousers?

MAN I'm not trying to break a world record. I took my trousers off to have a bath, and when I got out of the bath, my trousers were gone.

MICHAEL M I see. Get out of the way! We're on television!

The audience laugh.

V Sorry about that, ladies and gentlemen. Now back to Albert Hargreaves. Albert, you've been standing in that bucket of hot soup for seven hours and *two* minutes. Only *one* more minute to go, and you will break the world record. And here comes Mrs Hargreaves with more hot soup!

MRS HAR Here you are, Albert.

She pours some more soup into the bucket.

ALBERT Aaaargh!

MICHAEL M Tell me, Albert, how does it feel?

ALBERT Hot!

The audience laugh.

MICHAEL M No, no, no! How does it feel to be approaching the world record?

ALBERT Well, Michael, I've been dreaming about this moment, I've been thinking about nothing else –

MICHAEL M Yes, Albert.

ALBERT – I've been practising every day –

MICHAEL M Yes, Albert.

ALBERT *Twice* on Sundays!

MICHAEL M Yes – and here comes Mrs Hargreaves.

ALBERT Oh no, not again!

MICHAEL M It's all right, Albert, she's only looking at her watch!

The audience laugh.

MRS HAR Albert! Albert! Only ten seconds to go! Ten, nine, eight, seven –

Mabel pushes Albert.

MABEL (*Ironically:*) Congratulations, Albert!

ALBERT Aaaargh!

Albert falls over.

HILDA George, did you see that?

GEORGE No. What happened?

HILDA Mabel Phillips knocked him over with her brush!

MICHAEL M Well, ladies and gentlemen, Albert Hargreaves *hasn't* broken a world record, but he *has* broken . . . his leg!!

The programme ends.

Listening Comprehension

Questions

I 1 Had George and Hilda seen the TV programme before?
II 2 Do you think any of the people in the TV studio were well-known?
3 What was Albert Hargreaves trying to do?
4 Did Albert have a chance of being successful?
5 How did he keep the soup hot?
III 6 What is the world record for leaning on a brush?
7 Was Mabel Phillips close to breaking the record?
IV 8 Why did the 'young man' go on TV without his trousers?
V 9 Had Albert practised a lot?
10 Why didn't he break the world record?

In answering Question 2, the students should give reasons for thinking that Michael Moonshine was well-known: they may say, for instance, that the programme was probably a regular one, or that Albert Hargreaves called him 'Michael'. The important point about Question 8 is, of course, that the 'young man' did not realize he was on television. Question 9 elicits an answer in the Past Perfect Continuous tense, and the students can simply take Albert's remarks ('I've been practising every day' etc.) and replace 'I've . . .' with 'He had . . .'

Reading Comprehension

True or False?

On the day of the TV programme, the following 'preview' appeared in a newspaper. Was it an accurate 'preview'?

Your chance to break a world record *(BBC TV, 8 p.m.)*

The fascinating programme in which people try to break world records. Introduced by Michael Sunshine.
Tonight, Arnold Hargreaves will try to break the world record for standing in a bucket of hot water, and Muriel Phillips will try to hold a brush for longer than anyone else. She'll be there for quite a long time because the world record is more than two days! Arnold has been practising three times a week for his world record attempt.

There are several inaccuracies in the 'preview'. The students (either individually or in groups) should read the text, and note down the inaccuracies. Then the class as a whole can discuss them, and you may like to list them on the blackboard. A follow-up would then be to re-write the 'preview', making it accurate.

Word Puzzle

Look at the boxes below. Choose one word from each box, making sure that it fits with the words before and after. The words will form a question and there is only *one* possible correct question.

If	is	moon	try	at	eat	trees	?
Why	do	dog	enjoy	of	break	clouds	
Which	was	people	can	to	know	records	

When you have found the question, answer it.

The only possible question is 'Why do people try to break records?' (There are one or two rather interesting nonsensical possibilities, such as 'Why do people try to eat clouds?' and it may be amusing to comment on these in passing!) This is an easy puzzle, so you could make it a speed test: either ask the students, individually or in groups, to find the 'sensible' question as quickly as possible, or to find the 'sensible' questions plus three nonsensical questions as quickly as possible. When the students give their answers to the question, you could develop them into the discussion suggested on p. 88. ('What do you think?')

Communicating

Getting Information: Interviews

In the TV programme, Michael Moonshine interviewed people doing extraordinary things. He asked questions like:

> What is your name?
> What are you doing?
> How long have you been -ing . . .?
> What is the world record for -ing . . .?
> How does it feel to be -ing . . .?

In pairs, improvise dialogues between an interviewer and one of these people:

1 Someone sitting on top of a flagpole.
2 Someone walking from one end of the country to the other.
3 Someone trying to break the world record for eating eggs.
4 Someone preparing to walk across Niagara Falls on a tightrope.

The students can choose the roles they wish to play, or you can give them cue-cards (one card in each pair would simply read 'Interviewer' and the other would have one of the roles suggested above). Before the pairs begin their improvised dialogue, the 'interviewers' should prepare a few questions to ask, and the 'interviewees' should decide on a few details about their roles (e.g. name, length of time their activity has been going on, reasons for doing it, etc.). After a few minutes for this preparation, the students should improvise their 'interviews'. As a follow-up activity, some of the 'interviewers' can present their 'interviewees' to the rest of the class ('This is . . . He/She has been -ing for . . . , etc.), or the students can write newspaper articles based on their improvised dialogues.

In Your Own Words

Re-enact the sketch in your own words, without reading from the text. Do it in short sections. These words will remind you:

For re-enacting in the classroom, the first short section can be omitted, and the scene can open with the compère introducing the programme. Nothing is vital where 'props' are concerned: a pen or pencil or rolled paper can represent a microphone for the 'compère' to hold, 'Mabel Phillips' can lean on anything (a desk, for example), and needless to say, an actual bucket of hot soup is not required! The 'compère' and 'Mrs Hargreaves' should have watches to consult, but this can of course be mimed.

* Further Role-playing Activities

1 An Alternative Ending

The students can improvise the dialogue that would have taken place if Albert Hargreaves had broken the world record. Give different roles to students in groups: Albert, his wife, Michael Moonshine, Mabel Phillips, a journalist. Everyone should congratulate Albert and ask him how he feels. In addition, the journalist should ask Albert why he did it and what he's going to do next.

2 Introducing a TV Programme

Play the first part of Section II of the sketch again, to allow the students to hear Michael Moonshine beginning the TV programme. They can then work out their own introductions to these programmes:

1 *Twenty Questions* (where the contestants have to find out people's occupations).
2 *The £64,000 Game* (where people answer questions for money, with a top prize of £64,000).
3 *Star Quiz* (where famous people answer questions).
4 *Worth a Fortune* (where people guess the value of paintings, antiques, etc. and win prizes).
5 *Family Fun* (where members of the same family compete with each other for prizes).

In addition to what Michael Moonshine said, the following expressions may be useful:

Hello, and welcome once again to . . . .
We are very pleased to welcome (back) . . . .
For the benefit of new viewers, the idea of the game is . . . .
I'd like you to give a big round of applause to . . . .

The students can work in pairs to write their introductions, and when all the pairs have finished, one student from each pair can read the results to the class.
This could lead to a class game of Twenty Questions (See 'Gussett and Rose', Suggested Preliminary Practice, p. 16).

Pronunciation Practice

Unstressed Words

Replay to the students these lines from Section I of the sketch:

'Your chance to break a world record.'
'Oh, let's have a look at it.'

Point out that the 'weak vowel' /ə/ is used in the unimportant, unstressed words 'to' /tə/ and 'at' /ət/.
Then play Section II of the sketch, and ask the students to identify similar examples and imitate them. As the sound /ə/ is very frequent in English in unstressed syllables, there are quite a number of them: /tə/ənd/əv/fə/, for example, in:

'. . . meet them and see what they're doing.'
'. . . a bucket of hot soup.'
'. . . for six hours and fifty-eight minutes.'
'. . . four more minutes to go.'
'. . . that bucket of hot soup for almost seven hours now.'

Writing

A Newspaper Article

Write a short newspaper article, describing the events in the 'World Record' TV programme. First make notes on these points:

– Albert Hargreaves – his world record attempt – his preparation – his wife.
– Mabel Phillips – her world record attempt – her feelings.
– The other man's interruption.
– What Mabel did to Albert.

Then use your notes to write the article. Give it a headline, for example: WORLD RECORD ATTEMPT FAILS.

As with most writing exercises, this can be prepared by discussion in class in groups. The students should first make notes as suggested, and then combine their notes into the article, either in class or for homework. This narrative re-telling suggests the use of the Past Perfect Continuous ('Albert Hargreaves wanted to break the world record for standing on one leg in a bucket of hot soup. He *had been practising* very hard . . .' etc.). This tense parallels the Present Perfect Continuous practised in the sketch, and a few examples of its use could be given before the students begin the exercise.

What Do You Think?

The Olympic Games

Every four years, athletes try to break world records at the Olympic Games. Sometimes they only have ten seconds to prove they are the best in the world. The tension is terrible, and none of the athletes seem to be having a good time. Why do you think they do it? Are the Olympic Games a good thing?

The students can begin the discussion in two groups: one group should consider all arguments in favour of the Olympic Games, e.g. sporting achievements and bringing nations together. The other group should consider the arguments against, e.g. the expense and the political problems. After working out these arguments the students can then exchange the ideas produced with the class as a whole. They can then give their own personal feelings.

10

The Superlative Vacuum-cleaner

Whereas most sketches are given their first performance during the summer season in England, *The Superlative Vacuum-Cleaner* was first performed during a tour of Germany in May, 1974. The script given here is almost exactly the same as the stage version.
This sketch is suitable for Intermediate students and above.

Attitudes and Functions

Complaining
I detest my job. It's the most boring job in the world.

Advice and Suggestions
Your sales technique is all wrong. I'll show you. You come into the house and I'll ring the bell . . .

Surprise
You'll sell the vacuum-cleaner to *me*?

Complimenting
What a colourful carpet!
You're a fantastic saleswoman.

Sarcasm
Cleanest? Don't make me laugh!

Self-Criticism
I sometimes think I'm the worst vacuum-cleaner salesman in the world.

Structure and Usage

Main Point
Superlative of Adjectives
e.g. It's the quickest, the cleanest, the cheapest . . . the most economical, the most effective . . .

Other Points
Future Simple tense for Immediate Decision
e.g. I'll buy one.
I'll just go and get some money.
Exclamations
e.g. What a beautiful house you've got!
What a colourful carpet!

Note the Following Words and Expressions

dust superlative vacuum-cleaner smart economical effective revolutionary detest boring colourful carpet market (on the market) sales technique You've made the right decision.

Suggested Preliminary Practice

Probably the best introduction to this sketch is to show the students some advertisements from newspapers and magazines. Ask them to tell you what the 'selling point' is in each case. Choose advertisements which include expressions such as 'the cheapest . . .', 'the most comfortable . . .', 'the most exciting . . .' and so on. Ask the students whether they believe the advertisements.

Preliminary Questions

1 How did the salesman describe the vacuum-cleaner?
2 How did the housewife help him?
3 Do you think he was a good salesman?

10

The Superlative Vacuum-cleaner

SCENE	The hall of a house
CHARACTERS	A vacuum-cleaner salesman A housewife

I

The salesman rings the door-bell several times.

HOUSEWIFE Yes, I'm coming.

She opens the door.

Good morning.

SALESMAN Good morning, young lady. Is your mother in?

HOUSEWIFE My mother? I'm the mother in this house. What do you want?

SALESMAN Dust, madam.

HOUSEWIFE Dust?

SALESMAN Yes, madam. Dust.

HOUSEWIFE I haven't got any dust.

SALESMAN Oh yes you have!

He shakes dust onto the floor from a paper bag.

		All over your carpet!
	HOUSEWIFE	Hey! I've just cleaned this carpet! Why are you putting dust all over it?
	SALESMAN	Don't worry, madam. I've got the answer to all your problems *here*! The Superlative vacuum-cleaner!
	HOUSEWIFE	The Superlative vacuum-cleaner? Why's it called 'Superlative'?
	SALESMAN	Because, madam, everything about it *is* superlative. It's the quickest, the cleanest, the cheapest, the smallest, the smartest, the most economical, the most effective, the most beautiful, the most revolutionary vacuum-cleaner in the world. And it's only £65.
II	HOUSEWIFE	Are you trying to sell me a vacuum-cleaner?
	SALESMAN	Yes, madam.
	HOUSEWIFE	Well, go on, then.
	SALESMAN	I've finished, madam.
	HOUSEWIFE	Finished? You haven't said very much. What sort of a vacuum-cleaner salesman are you?
	SALESMAN	Not a very good one, I'm afraid.
	HOUSEWIFE	I can see that.
	SALESMAN	No, I'm a very *bad* vacuum-cleaner salesman. In fact, I'm the worst salesman in our company.
	HOUSEWIFE	The worst?
	SALESMAN	The worst. I sometimes think I'm the worst vacuum-cleaner salesman in the world.
	HOUSEWIFE	Oh, dear. Do you . . . like your job?
	SALESMAN	Like my job? No, madam. I detest my job. It's the most boring job in the world. Every day it's the same: 'Good morning, young lady. Is your mother in? . . . The Superlative vacuum-cleaner . . . The quickest, the cleanest, the cheapest, the smallest . . .'
	HOUSEWIFE	Well, *is* it the quickest?
	SALESMAN	No, it's probably the slowest.
	HOUSEWIFE	Is it the cleanest?
	SALESMAN	Cleanest? Don't make me laugh! I don't think there's a dirtier vacuum-cleaner on the market. And it certainly isn't the cheapest either.
III	HOUSEWIFE	No, no, no. This is no good at all.
	SALESMAN	Pardon?
	HOUSEWIFE	Look, do you want to sell this vacuum-cleaner or don't you?
	SALESMAN	I suppose so.
	HOUSEWIFE	Well, your sales technique is all wrong.
	SALESMAN	Is it?
	HOUSEWIFE	Yes. I could sell vacuum-cleaners better than you.
	SALESMAN	No, you couldn't.
	HOUSEWIFE	Yes, I could. I'll show you. You come into the house, and I'll ring the bell and sell the vacuum-cleaner to you.
	SALESMAN	*You'll* sell the vacuum-cleaner to *me*?
	HOUSEWIFE	Yes.
	SALESMAN	O.K. But it isn't as easy as you think.
	HOUSEWIFE	We'll see. Go inside and shut the door.

SALESMAN All right.

IV *The salesman goes into the house and closes the door. The housewife rings the bell. The salesman opens the door.*

SALESMAN Not today, thank you.

He closes the door. The housewife rings the bell again. The salesman opens the door again, and speaks in a high voice.

Yes?

HOUSEWIFE Hello!

SALESMAN Hello.

HOUSEWIFE My goodness me, what a beautiful house you've got!

SALESMAN Ooh, do you like it?

HOUSEWIFE Like it? It's the most beautiful house I've seen for a long time.

SALESMAN Thank you very much.

HOUSEWIFE May I come in?

SALESMAN Er . . .

HOUSEWIFE Thank you. Oh, what a colourful carpet!

SALESMAN Yes, it's lovely, isn't it?

HOUSEWIFE It's the most colourful carpet I've seen for ages. I should think it was very expensive.

SALESMAN The most expensive one in the shop.

HOUSEWIFE And I suppose you've got a very good vacuum-cleaner to look after it.

SALESMAN A vacuum-cleaner? No, I haven't.

HOUSEWIFE You haven't got a vacuum-cleaner?

SALESMAN No.

HOUSEWIFE Well, madam, this is your lucky day, because I have *here* the best vacuum-cleaner that money can buy: the Superlative vacuum-cleaner.

SALESMAN Is it really good?

HOUSEWIFE Good? Good? It's the . . . the . . .

SALESMAN (*In his own voice:*) Quickest.

HOUSEWIFE . . . the quickest, the . . .

SALESMAN Cleanest.

HOUSEWIFE . . . the cleanest, the cheapest, the smallest, the smartest, the most economical, the most effective, the most beautiful, the most revolutionary vacuum-cleaner in the world.

SALESMAN (*In a high voice again:*) Ooh! How much is it?

HOUSEWIFE Just £65 to you, madam.

SALESMAN I'll buy one.

HOUSEWIFE Good.

SALESMAN (*In his own voice:*) Er . . . where's the money?

HOUSEWIFE It's in my handbag on the kitchen table.

SALESMAN Oh, right. (*In the high voice:*) I'll just go and get some money.

He goes to the kitchen to get the money.

HOUSEWIFE Good idea, madam. You've made the right decision.

The salesman comes back, speaking in his own voice.

SALESMAN	Do you know, you're a fantastic saleswoman.
HOUSEWIFE	Ooh!
SALESMAN	You've got a fantastic sales technique.
HOUSEWIFE	Do you think so?
SALESMAN	Yes, you've got the best sales technique I've seen all day.
HOUSEWIFE	Thank you!
SALESMAN	Thank *you*, madam.
	He leaves and closes the door.
	(*Speaking to himself, counting the money:*) Ten, twenty, thirty, forty, fifty, sixty, sixty-five. Now *that's* the way to sell a vacuum-cleaner.

Listening Comprehension

Questions

I 1 Why did the salesman say: 'Is your mother in?'
2 Why did he put dust on the carpet?
3 Why was the vacuum-cleaner called the 'Superlative' vacuum-cleaner?

II 4 Did the housewife think he was a good salesman?
5 Did the salesman think he was good?
6 How did he describe his job?

III 7 What did the housewife think his problem was?
8 What did she suggest?

IV 9 How did the housewife begin her 'sales talk'?
10 Did the salesman sell the vacuum-cleaner?

In answering Question 1, the students should comment on the fact that the salesman wanted to flatter the housewife by suggesting that she was the daughter of the house, rather than the mother. (Unfortunately for him, it didn't work as she wasn't flattered.) Question 5 may provoke some discussion: in section II of the sketch, the salesman criticizes himself, but at the end we realize that it was part of his plan, and he in fact *compliments* himself.

Reading Comprehension

What Happened Next?

Read these four possible continuations of the sketch. Choose the one which you think is most probable.

1 The housewife was delighted with her new vacuum-cleaner. She tried it immediately and it worked very well. She telephoned her husband at his office, to tell him that she had spent some of their holiday money.
2 The housewife went back into the kitchen. Suddenly she realized what she had done. She had bought a vacuum-cleaner that she didn't want, and she had spent £65 of her holiday money. 'Oh, well,' she said, 'at least I helped someone today.' She made herself a cup of tea.
3 The housewife realized what she had done immediately. She opened the door and ran down the garden path. The salesman was getting into his car. 'Just a minute,' said the housewife, 'I want my money back.' 'All right,' said the salesman, 'Here you are. £65.'
4 When the housewife realized what she had done, she opened the door and called to the salesman. 'I don't want this vacuum-cleaner,' she said. 'Give me my money back.' 'I'm sorry,' said the salesman. 'You've got the vacuum-cleaner, and I've got the money.' The housewife was furious: 'I'm going to call the police,' she said.

The students should read the four possible continuations silently to themselves, and then discuss in small groups which one they would choose and why. (In discussing their choices, they can comment on the characteristics which would make each one possible: for example, if the housewife was a very kind but naive person, No. 2 would be possible; if the salesman regretted having played a trick on the housewife, No. 3 would be possible.) The class as a whole can discuss the choices of the students in the groups.

Word Puzzle

What are the opposites of the words below? (The answers were all used in the sketch.)

ugliest 1 _ _ _ _ / ☐ _ _ _ _ _ _ _ _
most expensive 2 _ _ _ ☐ _ _ _ _
most untidy 3 _ _ _ ☐ _ _ _ _

biggest 4 _ _ ☐ _ _ _ _ _
noisiest 5 _ _ ☐ _ _ _ _ _
dirtiest 6 _ _ _ _ ☐ _ _ _

Put the boxed letters in these boxes:

1 2 3 4 5 6

☐ ☐ ☐ ☐ ☐ ☐ ☐

There is one letter missing. Here is a clue to it: In the sketch, the housewife asked: 'What sort of a vacuum-cleaner salesman are you?' Read the salesman's answer. The missing letter is the *first* letter of one of the words in his answer.
What does the word in the boxes mean?

Solution: 1 most beautiful 2 cheapest 3 smartest 4 smallest 5 quietest 6 cleanest. The letters in the boxes are therefore: 1–B, 2–A, 3–R, 4–A, 5–I, 6–N. The missing letter is 'G' – the first letter of the word 'good' in the salesman's line 'Not a very good one, I'm afraid.' The word in the boxes is therefore 'bargain', something (like the vacuum-cleaner?) which seems to be good value.

Communicating

1 *Complimenting*

Listen to the first half of section IV of the sketch again. Notice how the housewife, as a saleswoman, says complimentary things about the house:

What a beautiful house you've got!
It's the most beautiful house I've seen for a long time.
Oh, what a colourful carpet!

Practise in pairs, complimenting and accepting compliments about clothes. Use these expressions:

Your (dress) is really lovely.	Thank you.
It's a beautiful colour.	Oh, do you like it?
It really suits you.	It's very nice of you to say so.
It fits you perfectly.	Do you think so?

You can also practise complimenting someone on: their new car, a painting they have done, their garden.

2 *Persuading Someone to Buy Something*

If you want to sell something, you have to say how good it is. (Remember how the salesman described the vacuum-cleaner.) Practise selling things to one another. You can use anything: pens, books, watches, rings, etc. Practise in pairs. The 'salesman' can use some expressions from the first list; the 'customer' can use some expressions from the second list.

It's as good as new.	I don't really need one.
I've only had it for a few weeks.	I'm not sure.
It works perfectly.	I'll think about it.
I've hardly used it.	It looks like a bargain.
They're much more expensive these days.	It's a bit expensive.
I'll let you have it half price.	O.K. I'll take it.

Exercise 1: Play the appropriate section of the sketch again, and point out the compliments. Then give an example of a short dialogue based on the expressions given in the two boxes, and allow the students to practise in pairs. Any of the replies can be used with compliments of the types given in the first box.
Exercise 2: Take one of your own possessions, and try to 'sell' it to members of the class, mentioning its advantages, using expressions from the first list. Then practise the possible replies from the second list with the class as a whole, before letting the students practise in pairs. After the oral practice in pairs, the students, still in pairs, could write short dialogues incorporating the expressions.

In Your Own Words

Re-enact the sketch in your own words, without reading from the text. Do it in short sections. These words will remind you:

For simple re-enacting of this sketch in the classroom, any object can be used to represent the vacuum-cleaner (for example, a wastepaper basket, a pile of books, a bag); of course, as with all the sketches, it can be done purely in mime, with no 'props' at all, but it helps to have something for the 'salesman' to refer to, point to, hold up, etc. as he extols its virtues. Some folded paper can be used to represent the money. Encourage the students to make the situation clear by their movements: ringing the door-bell, opening the door, changing places at the appropriate times, and so on.

Further Role-playing Activities

Situations Parallel to the Sketch
Organize activities for role-playing in which the characters change roles, as the housewife and the salesman did in the sketch. For example: A policeman stops a motorist to ask him why he was driving so fast. The policeman is not very competent, and the motorist offers to ask the questions. The dialogue might start like this:

Policeman : You were driving too fast.
Motorist : That's right.
Policeman : Ah.
Motorist : Well, go on, then.
Policeman : Go on? I've finished.
Motorist : What sort of a policeman are you?
Policeman : Not a very good one, I'm afraid.
Motorist : Look, you get into the car, and I'll ask the questions.
. . . .

Try to devise enough activities for all the students to be involved, either in pairs or in groups. Here are some more possibilities:

1 A salesman in a shop and a customer. It can be a shop selling clothes, shoes, furniture, cars, etc.
2 A policeman giving directions to a tourist.
3 A manager explaining a job to a new employee.
4 A geography teacher and a pupil who knows more about geography.

* Pronunciation Practice

Sarcasm
Replay the final lines of section II of the sketch, and draw the students' attention to the salesman's sarcastic reply:

'Cleanest? Don't make me laugh!'

The students should listen carefully to the stress and intonation in this response, and then suggest similar responses to these questions:

1 Is your old car running well?
2 Was the food good while you were on holiday?
3 Did the boss give you more money?
4 Is your new watch made of gold?
5 Can you change a £20 note for me?

Make sure that they choose the key words for their replies (i.e. 1 'Running well?'; 2 'Good?'; 3 'More money?'; 4 'Gold?' or 'Made of gold?'; 5 'A £20 note?').
They could also use these expressions (instead of 'Don't make me laugh!'):

You must be joking!
You can't be serious!
Some hope!

Point out to the students that the sarcasm here is really quite mild. It is, in fact, slightly humorous and not at all offensive, although it could only be used when the two speakers know each other well.
Note: The aim of this exercise is that the students should recognize the tone of the replies and should not necessarily be expected to reproduce them exactly.

Writing

An Advertisement
Look at this advertisement for a car, and then write your own advertisement for the Superlative vacuum-cleaner.

Ask the students to 'design' the advertisement, i.e. to set it out rather like the example, rather than just writing several sentences. This exercise would make a good homework assignment, as it is fairly controlled but leaves room for imagination as well. Alternatively, it could be done as a group activity in class, and if done in this way different groups could work on different products or all groups could work on the vacuum-cleaner.

What Do You Think?

Advertisements

We are surrounded by advertisements and people trying to sell us things. We see advertisements on TV, in the street and in the newspapers. Sometimes, people come to the door and try to sell us things.
Do we need so much advertising? Wouldn't it be better if we could choose what we wanted, without all the advertisements and salesmen?

* You might start this discussion by showing the students some advertisements from newspapers and magazines, as suggested in the 'Preliminary Practice' on p. 89. Give one or two advertisements to each group of students, and ask them to discuss them: Which do they like? Why? Which do they dislike? Why? They can also discuss in their groups the advantages and disadvantages of advertisements. The groups' views can then be discussed with the class as a whole. For a follow-up session, the students could bring in examples of advertisements which they consider particularly good or particularly bad, and present them to the class with their comments.

11

Superman and the Psychiatrist

This sketch was first performed in 1975, and the text here is a shortened version of that used on stage. On stage, *Superman* achieved success as a pop star, singing with a rather intense electric guitarist and three dancing vocalists providing the accompaniment, the whole ensemble wearing shiny silver jackets. This ending has been modified here.

This sketch is suitable for Intermediate students and above.

Attitudes and Functions

Asking for Advice

What can I do?
What do you think?
Do you think it's a good idea?

Giving Advice and Making Suggestions

I think you should change your job.
You could get a job as an English teacher.

Polite, Businesslike Forms

Do sit down.
What seems to be the trouble?
Come this way, please.

Predicting

I'll lose my job.
I can see it all now. Your name will be in lights!

Structure and Usage

Main Point

Ability and Possibility: 'can'/'can't'/'could'/'couldn't'.
e.g. If you can't fly, you can't be Superman.
In the old days . . . I could run into a telephone-box . . .

Other Points

Present Perfect tense
e.g. How long have you been like this?
I've changed my mind.

Relative clauses
e.g. No-one wants a man who can only shout.
Oh, I see . . . someone who *thinks* he's Superman.

Note the Following Words and Expressions

shout library, librarian contract Sorry to trouble you. What seems to be the trouble? In that case, . . . It took me (15 minutes) to . . . (name) in lights In the old days, . . .

Note: Rather than teaching the word 'librarian' beforehand, you may like to let the students deduce its meaning from the context if it is a new word. This will avoid pre-empting the joke.

Suggested Preliminary Practice

Preliminary practice could focus on the giving of advice using the expression 'I think you should . . .'. Present the students with some 'dilemmas' and ask them for their advice ('What should I do?'). The dilemmas could be, for example:

1 I found a £5 note in the street this morning.
2 I don't earn enough money in this job.
3 The postman always reads my letters.
4 My new shirt came to pieces in the washing-machine.

Note: It is also useful, before the students listen to the sketch, to make sure that they know something about Superman (his abilities, his changing from a 'normal' person into Superman).

Preliminary Questions

1 Why did Mr Wilkins go to see the psychiatrist?
2 Did Superman have the same type of problem?
3 How did the psychiatrist solve their problems?

11

Superman and the Psychiatrist

SCENE	A psychiatrist's consulting-room
CHARACTERS	A psychiatrist Angela, the psychiatrist's receptionist Mr Wilkins Superman

I

The receptionist comes in.

PSYCHIATRIST Who's next, Angela?

RECEPTIONIST There's a man to see you, doctor. His name is Wilkins. He says he can't talk quietly. He can only shout.

Mr Wilkins shouts from outside the door.

MR WILKINS Can I come in?!!

PSYCHIATRIST Hmm. Yes, I see. Ask him to come in.

RECEPTIONIST Come in, Mr Wilkins.

MR WILKINS Thank you!!

He comes in. The receptionist goes out.

Hello, doctor. Sorry to trouble you.

PSYCHIATRIST That's all right, Mr Wilkins. Do sit down.

Mr Wilkins sits down.

II Now . . . what seems to be the trouble?

MR WILKINS Well, doctor, I can't talk quietly. I can only shout.

PSYCHIATRIST (*Shouting:*) How long have you been like this?

MR WILKINS Pardon?

PSYCHIATRIST (*Back to normal:*) How long have you been like this?

MR WILKINS About a week.

PSYCHIATRIST Well, don't worry. I think you've got a very nice shouting voice.

MR WILKINS But I can't go on like this. I'll lose my job.

PSYCHIATRIST What *is* your job?

MR WILKINS I'm a librarian. I work in a library. I can't shout at work, you know.

PSYCHIATRIST In that case, Mr Wilkins, I think you should change your job.

MR WILKINS But what can I do? No-one wants a man who can only shout.

PSYCHIATRIST You could get a job as an English teacher.

MR WILKINS An English teacher?

PSYCHIATRIST Yes, they shout all the time.

MR WILKINS All right, doctor. I'll do that. Goodbye.

PSYCHIATRIST Goodbye, Mr Wilkins.

He leaves, still shouting.

MR WILKINS Hey, you! Write down this verb!

RECEPTIONIST Goodbye, Mr Wilkins.

The receptionist comes back into the room.

Is Mr Wilkins all right, doctor?

PSYCHIATRIST Yes. He's going to be an English teacher.

RECEPTIONIST Oh.

III PSYCHIATRIST Who's next?

RECEPTIONIST Superman.

PSYCHIATRIST Superman?

RECEPTIONIST Yes.

PSYCHIATRIST Oh, I see . . . someone who *thinks* he's Superman.

RECEPTIONIST No, doctor. He really *is* Superman.

PSYCHIATRIST What? The big, strong man who flies through the air?

RECEPTIONIST Yes.

PSYCHIATRIST Oh, I see. Ask him to come in.

RECEPTIONIST Yes, doctor. (*To Superman:*) Come this way, please.

Superman comes in, very tired and out-of-breath.

SUPERMAN Thank you.

PSYCHIATRIST Thank you, Angela.

The receptionist goes out.

Good morning, Mr . . . er . . .

SUPERMAN Superman.

PSYCHIATRIST Yes, Superman. Do sit down.

Superman sits down.

SUPERMAN Thank you.

PSYCHIATRIST	Well, what seems to be the trouble?
SUPERMAN	Well, doctor, I'm Superman. People think I can do everything, but I can't. I can't do *anything* any more.
PSYCHIATRIST	What can't you do?
SUPERMAN	I can't climb buildings, I can't lift cars . . . and I can't fly.
PSYCHIATRIST	Well, don't worry. A lot of people have that problem.
SUPERMAN	But you don't understand. I'm Superman. If you can't fly, you can't be Superman. It's in the contract.
PSYCHIATRIST	Ah yes, I see.
SUPERMAN	In the old days, when people called for Superman, I could run into a telephone-box, take off my boring grey city suit, and become Superman, all in ten seconds. Yesterday, I went into a telephone-box, and it took me fifteen minutes just to take off my trousers. And when I came out, I couldn't remember where I was going. What do you think of that?
	The psychiatrist is asleep.
	Eh?

IV PSYCHIATRIST (*Waking up:*) What? Pardon?

SUPERMAN What do you think?

PSYCHIATRIST I think you should change your job.

SUPERMAN But what can I do?

PSYCHIATRIST Well, you've got a very nice face. You could be a pop singer.

SUPERMAN A pop singer?

PSYCHIATRIST Yes. Can you sing?

SUPERMAN No, I can't.

PSYCHIATRIST Can you dance?

SUPERMAN No.

PSYCHIATRIST Can you play the guitar?

SUPERMAN No.

PSYCHIATRIST So – you can't sing, you can't dance, and you can't play the guitar.

SUPERMAN That's right.

PSYCHIATRIST Well, you could be an *excellent* pop singer.

SUPERMAN What?

PSYCHIATRIST Yes, I can see it all now. Your name will be in lights! You'll be famous!

SUPERMAN But I *am* famous. I'm *Superman*.

PSYCHIATRIST Not any more. From today, you are Rocky Superdazzle!

SUPERMAN Do you think it's a good idea?

PSYCHIATRIST Yes, of course . . . Rocky.

V *The receptionist comes in again.*

RECEPTIONIST Doctor –

PSYCHIATRIST Yes, Angela?

RECEPTIONIST – Mr Wilkins is back again.

Mr Wilkins comes in, shouting as before.

MR WILKINS Yes, I am. I've changed my mind. I don't want to be an English teacher. What else can I do?

PSYCHIATRIST Don't worry, Mr Wilkins. I've got another job for you. You can work with Rocky Superdazzle here.

SUPERMAN How do you do?

MR WILKINS Rocky Superdazzle? That's not Rocky Superdazzle! That's Superman. I saw him in a telephone-box yesterday. Superman! Huh! It took him fifteen minutes just to take off his trousers.

PSYCHIATRIST Well, he *was* Superman, but he's not Superman any more. I think you can both work together . . .

A few weeks later, at a pop concert.

MR WILKINS Ladies and gentlemen, you've heard of Rod Stewart! You've heard of Mick Jagger! You've heard of Queen Elizabeth the Second of England! Well, tonight we present a new star on the pop scene. He's *sexier* than Rod Stewart! He's *wilder* than Mick Jagger! And he's . . . *taller* than Queen Elizabeth the Second of England! Ladies and gentlemen – Rocky Superdazzle!

The audience screams and applauds.

SUPERMAN Thank you! Thank you very much! Thank you!

Listening Comprehension

Questions

I 1 Was Mr Wilkins the psychiatrist's first patient that day?
II 2 Why was Mr Wilkins worried about his job?
3 What job did the psychiatrist suggest for Mr Wilkins?
III 4 Why was Superman worried about his job?
5 What happened to Superman the day before he saw the psychiatrist?
6 Why did the psychiatrist fall asleep?
IV 7 Why did the psychiatrist tell Superman to become a pop singer?
8 Name three things that Superman couldn't do.
V 9 Why did Mr Wilkins come back?
10 Had Mr Wilkins met Superman before?

The clue to the answer to Question 1 is in the very first line of the sketch, where the psychiatrist asks: 'Who's next, Angela?' Obviously there had been someone before Mr Wilkins. In answering Question 5, the students should give the gist of Superman's lengthy speech in their own words. The answer to Question 7 could simply be 'Because he had a very nice face', although the students may like to add that the psychiatrist believes that pop singers don't need to sing, dance or play the guitar very well. For Question 10, it should be said that Mr Wilkins had *seen* Superman before, but it is not possible to say with certainty that he had *met* him before.

Reading Comprehension

Read and Complete

Read these three possible continuations of the sketch, and put in the missing words.

1 Superman kept his (1) . . . . . . name, and was a great success (2) . . . . . . a pop singer. He and his (3) . . . . . ., the Supermen, had twenty hit records (4) . . . . . . their first year. His voice was (5) . . . . . . terrible, but he (6) . . . . . . a fortune. People bought millions (7) . . . . . . his records. He was most (8) . . . . . . in America and Scotland.

2 Superman (9) . . . . . . a record: 'What can I do?' by the Rocky Superdazzle Band. No-one bought it (10) . . . . . . his mother. She only (11) . . . . . . to it once, because his (12) . . . . . . was absolutely terrible. Quite a (13) . . . . . . of people came to his first concert, but (14) . . . . . . twelve came to his second. No-one at (15) . . . . . . came to his third. He (16) . . . . . . a bank clerk.

3 Superman got a contract (17) . . . . . . a record company. (The publicity manager (18) . . . . . . the company liked his face). He took singing (19) . . . . . . and improved his voice. At (20) . . . . . ., he wasn't very successful, and only sang (21) . . . . . . small clubs. A year later, he (22) . . . . . . on TV, and suddenly everyone wanted (23) . . . . . . records. In fact, the records were very good.

Which continuation do you like best? Why?

The answers are: 1 new 2 as 3 group/band/musicians 4 in/during 5 absolutely/really 6 made 7 of 8 popular/successful/famous 9 made 10 except/except for 11 listened 12 voice/singing 13 lot/number 14 only 15 all 16 became 17 with 18 of 19 lessons 20 first 21 in 22 appeared/sang 23 his

Word Puzzle

All the answers in this puzzle begin with the letter 'S'.

1 Mr Wilkins couldn't . . . . at work because he was a librarian.
2 When Mr Wilkins came into the psychiatrist's room, he said: '. . . . . to trouble you.'

3 The psychiatrist asked: 'What . . . . to be the trouble?'
4 The psychiatrist thought Mr Wilkins . . . . change his job.
5 The second patient wasn't . . . . who thought he was Superman – he *was* Superman.
6 Superman wasn't . . . . any more. He couldn't lift cars or climb buildings.
7 He became a pop . . . .

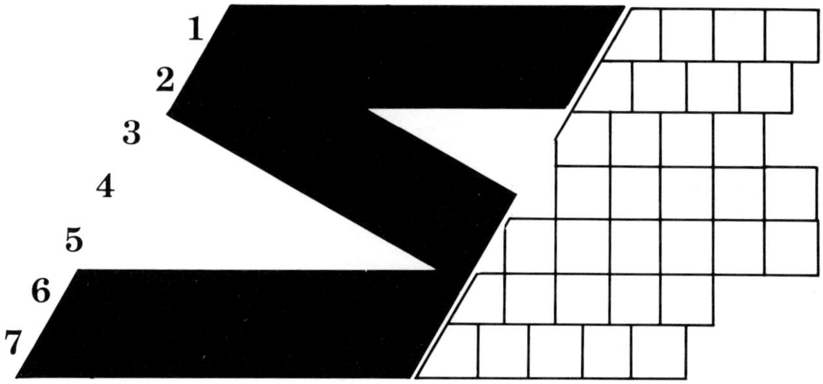

Solution: 1 shout 2 sorry 3 seems 4 should 5 someone 6 strong 7 singer.

Communicating

1 Making Suggestions
In the sketch, the psychiatrist made some suggestions for jobs:

– to Mr Wilkins: You could get a job as an English teacher.
– to Superman: You could be a pop singer.

This form ('You could . . .') is an informal way of making suggestions. It is especially useful if you want to make several suggestions:

You could . . . or you could . . . or you could always* . . .

* You add 'always' to your final suggestion if you don't think it is as good as the others.
Make suggestions to the people who have these problems:

1 There are no trains. How can I get to work?
2 I've won £1,000, and I don't know what to do with it.
3 Anna's phone is out of order. How can I contact her?
4 My neighbour always parks his lorry in front of my garage.

2 Predicting
Both Mr Wilkins and the psychiatrist spoke about the future:

I can't go on like this. I'll lose my job. I can see it all now. Your name will be in lights! You'll be famous!

Continue these sentences with predictions:

1 Don't put boiling water in that glass. . . . .
2 I don't think you should give your grandfather a Rocky Superdazzle T-shirt for his birthday. . . . .
3 Don't leave that box in front of the door. . . . .
4 You shouldn't work so hard. . . . .

Exercise 1: This can be done in pairs, with one student stating the problem and the other student making several suggestions. The suggestion which includes the word 'always' should be less confidently stated than the others; for example: No. 1. might be 'You could catch a bus . . . or you could take a taxi . . . or you could always *walk*.' (When suggestions are made in this way, the word 'Well, . . .' often prefaces the first one, and the final, more tentative suggestion is often stressed quite heavily.)*
Exercise 2: Note that a prediction with a negative ('won't') is most likely in No. 2 (e.g. 'He won't like it', 'He won't wear it').
* Other ways of making suggestions are practised in 'Communicating', Exercise 1 on p. 115 ('How about/What about . . . ?')

In Your Own Words

Re-enact the sketch in your own words, without reading from the text. Do it in short sections. These words will remind you:

For re-enacting this sketch, it is useful for the psychiatrist to sit at a desk, with a chair for the patients (Mr Wilkins and then Superman). 'Superman' should be very tired and depressed, and move and speak accordingly. All the 'characters' should be encouraged to mime the opening and closing of the door as they come in and out. For a more elaborate 'performance' than simple classroom re-enacting, the following 'props' will be useful: a white coat and perhaps glasses for the 'psychiatrist', a T-shirt with a large 'S' on it and an old coat or mackintosh for 'Superman', and even a psychiatrist's couch (with the patients being asked to lie down rather than sit down, although they should not remain lying down for long or the effect of their lines will be lost).

Further Role-playing Activities

Giving Advice

This activity is an extension of that suggested for Preliminary Practice (p. 99). The students practice asking for advice and giving advice in pairs. One student in each pair has a cue-card, setting out a problem, for example:

> You are a policeman.
> You haven't got very much money, and you have a lot of debts.
> A criminal has offered you £500 if you don't arrest him.

> You are an architect.
> Someone has offered you a very good job in another country.
> You will have to stay there for two years.
> You want to go, but your family don't like the idea.

The student should explain the problem and ask for advice. The other student should offer advice, and can make use of expressions such as: 'I think you should . . .', 'You could . . .'. The pairs can be expanded to threes or fours, so that the student with the 'problem' receives advice from several different people at the same time; this should produce some discussion. After a while, the cue-cards can be moved to different groups, giving each group several 'problems' to deal with.

Pronunciation Practice

Stress

Replay to the students these lines from section II of the sketch, pointing out and practising the stressed 'is':

Mr Wilkins : But I can't go on like this. I'll lose my job.
Psychiatrist : What *is* your job?
Mr Wilkins : I'm a librarian.

Then play the first half of section III, the second half of section IV and the first half of section V, asking the students to find three similar examples. There is one example in each section:

III No, doctor. He really *is* Superman.
IV But I *am* famous.
V Well, he *was* Superman, but he's not Superman any more.

Stressed forms – 'is' rather than ''s', 'am' rather than ''m', /wɔz/ rather than /wəz/ – are used in these examples for emphasis ('He really *is* Superman', 'But I *am* famous') or for contrastive purposes ('Well, he *was* Superman . . .'). These stressed forms would always be used in short answers, e.g. 'Yes, it is,' 'Yes, I am.' 'Yes, it was.' etc.

Writing

A Newspaper Article

When Superman became a pop singer, a journalist interviewed him and wrote an article about him. These are the questions which the journalist asked Superman:

Write answers to the questions (in notes). Then write the newspaper article. It could begin like this:

SUPERMAN BECOMES POP SINGER
Superman is not Superman any more.
He is now Rocky Superdazzle. . . . .

Include some quotations from Superman.

This exercise could be done in pairs in class, or notes could be made in class and written up for homework. The quotations from Superman can be given in Direct Speech ('I was unhappy as Superman,' he said, 'because I couldn't climb buildings or fly any more.' etc.) or, if the students are familiar with it, in Reported Speech (He told me he was unhappy as Superman . . .). The students should include as many facts from the sketch as they like, and feel free to add other details of their own.

What Do You Think?

Pop Singers

'Pop singers have a very easy life, and earn far too much money.' 'It's a hard life, being a pop singer.' What do you think? Would you like to be a pop singer?

The students can discuss this topic in small groups, examining the advantages and disadvantages of being a pop singer. Each group can have a 'secretary' who notes down the ideas raised (in two columns). After discussing the pros and cons, the students can give their own reasons for liking or disliking the idea of being a pop singer. Following the discussion in groups, the class as a whole can compare their findings.

12
The Travel Agency

Like *Gussett and Rose*, this sketch began as a dialogue written for the Belgian magazine 'English Pages'. It was adapted for the ETT's stage-show, and first performed in July 1975. In the stage version, the travel agent used a large number of 'visual aids', among them a rubber snake, a toy parachute and a reversible diagram of the Sahara Desert and the Arctic Ocean, in order to illustrate the holidays he was offering; the script has therefore been slightly adapted for this book. The sketch has been televised in Holland.
This sketch is suitable for Intermediate and more Advanced students as there is quite a heavy vocabulary load.

Attitudes and Functions

Making Suggestions
How about the Sahara Desert?
How about two weeks in Brighton?

Polite Requests
We'd like some information about holidays.
Could you just sign this form?

Surprise
By parachute?!

Relief
Well, at least you get a map.

Polite/Abrupt Refusals
I don't think we'd like that.
No, thanks!

'Presenting the Facts'
There are sandstorms nearly every day. . . . Sandstorms, dangerous snakes, and, on the last day, a stampede of camels!

Structure and Usage

Main Point
The Present Perfect tense
e.g. Have you been to Brighton? – No, we haven't.
Have you ever seen a frightened camel?

Other Points
Comparisons
e.g. You want something cheaper.
£600! It's still much too expensive for us.

Participles
e.g. . . . ten days in Paris – painting the outside of the Eiffel Tower.

Note the Following Words and Expressions
fish and chip shop sandstorm stampede parachute the Sahara Desert the Arctic Ocean the Amazon jungle the Eiffel Tower bull-fighting a holiday to remember

Suggested Preliminary Practice
The distinction between the Present Perfect tense and the Past Simple tense when referring to past experiences often remains a problem even for fairly advanced students. This sketch provides a large number of examples of the Present Perfect tense, and some preliminary practice contrasting the two tenses is useful.
This could be done by building up a series of examples of people and places they have visited. For instance:

Fred	Paris	1964
Mary	Hamburg	1973
Anne	Cairo	1969

A table with the information can be put on the blackboard, and comments made first in the Past Simple tense ('X went to Y in 19—', 'When did X visit Y?' etc.).
The time references can then be removed, or a different set of people and places provided, so that the Present Perfect tense would be appropriate. For example:

Jack/Berlin	YES
Diana/Tokyo	NO
Tony/Madrid	YES

('X has been to Y', 'Has X visited Y?' etc.).
Note: Without giving away too much about the sketch, it is advisable to make sure that the students know the places referred to: the Sahara Desert, the Amazon jungle, and so on.

Preliminary Questions
1 Who did the travel agent speak to on the telephone?
2 What kind of holiday did the customers want?
3 Which holiday did they book?

12

The Travel Agency

SCENE — A travel agency in London

CHARACTERS — A travel agent
Martin and Brenda Spencer

I

The travel agent is sitting at his desk in the travel agency. The phone rings.

TRAVEL AGENT (*On the telephone:*) Honest Harry's Happy Holidays. Can I help you? . . . Oh, it's *you*, sir. . . . This is Perkins speaking, yes. . . . The holidays in Brighton? Well, I haven't sold very many . . . I'm doing my best, but people aren't interested in Brighton these days. . . . My job? Yes, I *do* like my job . . . Yes, I *do* want to *keep* my job. . . . Yes, sir. All right, I'll sell some holidays in Brighton. Yes, sir. Yes, sir. Goodbye.

He puts the phone down.

Oh, dear.

II *Martin and Brenda come in.*

MARTIN Go on, Brenda.

BRENDA Excuse me, is this a travel agency?

TRAVEL AGENT No, madam. It's a fish and chip shop.

BRENDA Oh, sorry. Come on, Martin.

TRAVEL AGENT No, no, this *is* a travel agency. Just a little joke.

BRENDA Oh.

TRAVEL AGENT Yes, welcome to Honest Harry's Happy Holidays. Do sit down.

BRENDA Thank you.

MARTIN Thank you.

They sit down.

III TRAVEL AGENT What can I do for you?

BRENDA We'd like some information about holidays.

TRAVEL AGENT Oh, good.

MARTIN Yes, we'd like to go somewhere interesting.

TRAVEL AGENT Somewhere interesting? Have you been to Brighton?

MARTIN Brighton? No, we haven't –

TRAVEL AGENT Really?

BRENDA – and we don't want to, either.

TRAVEL AGENT Why not?

MARTIN Well, it's not *exciting*. We want to go somewhere *exciting*.

TRAVEL AGENT I see. How about the Sahara Desert?

BRENDA The Sahara Desert?

TRAVEL AGENT Yes. Have you ever been there?

MARTIN No, we haven't.

TRAVEL AGENT Well, this is the holiday for you. Forty-five days in the middle of the Sahara Desert.

BRENDA In the middle of the Sahara Desert? Is there anything to do?

TRAVEL AGENT Oh yes, there's plenty to do. Have you ever been in a sandstorm?

MARTIN A sandstorm? No, we haven't.

TRAVEL AGENT Oh well, it's very exciting. There are sandstorms nearly every day. And lots of dangerous snakes. Have you ever been bitten by a dangerous snake?

MARTIN }
BRENDA } No!

TRAVEL AGENT Oh well, it's very exciting.

BRENDA No, I don't think we'd like –

TRAVEL AGENT Sandstorms, dangerous snakes, and, on the last day, a stampede of camels!

MARTIN A stampede of camels? What's that?

TRAVEL AGENT Haven't you ever seen a stampede of camels?

MARTIN No.

TRAVEL AGENT Oh, it's very exciting. You stand in the middle of three hundred camels, someone fires a gun in the air – Bang! – and all the camels get frightened and run away.

BRENDA With us standing in the middle?

TRAVEL AGENT Yes. Have you ever seen a frightened camel?

BRENDA No. Is it exciting?

TRAVEL AGENT Exciting? It's terrifying!

MARTIN Isn't it dangerous?

TRAVEL AGENT Of course it's dangerous! That's what makes it exciting!

MARTIN Er . . . how much is it?

TRAVEL AGENT £800.

BRENDA £800!

TRAVEL AGENT And £5 extra for the stampede of camels.

BRENDA That's very expensive.

IV TRAVEL AGENT Ah, I see. You want something cheaper. Um . . . how about the Arctic Ocean? Have you ever been to the Arctic?

MARTIN No, we haven't.

TRAVEL AGENT Well, we can give you three weeks in a small boat in the Arctic Ocean. Each boat has a small hole in the bottom –

BRENDA A hole in the bottom?

TRAVEL AGENT – and you have enough food for ten days.

MARTIN Ten days?

TRAVEL AGENT That's right.

MARTIN But the holiday is for three weeks.

TRAVEL AGENT That's what makes it exciting! And it's only £600.

BRENDA £600! It's still much too expensive for us.

MARTIN Have you got anything a little bit cheaper?

TRAVEL AGENT Cheaper . . . well, I don't know. Let me see . . . Oh, yes. Now *this* is a holiday to remember. The Amazon jungle. Have you been to the Amazon jungle?

MARTIN No, we haven't.

TRAVEL AGENT Well, this may be the holiday for you. We drop you into the middle of the Amazon jungle by parachute –

MARTIN By parachute!

TRAVEL AGENT Yes, we drop you into the middle of the Amazon jungle, with a map –

BRENDA Well, at least you get a map.

TRAVEL AGENT – with a map of the London Underground.

BRENDA Oh. I don't think we'd like that. It sounds very dangerous.

TRAVEL AGENT Yes, but it's very *exciting*! This is the twentieth century. People want exciting holidays. *You* said *you* wanted an exciting holiday.

MARTIN But all your holidays are dangerous, expensive, and too far away from home.

TRAVEL AGENT Oh, I see. Now you want something nearer home.

MARTIN Er . . . yes.

V TRAVEL AGENT Have you ever been to Spain?

MARTIN No, we haven't.

TRAVEL AGENT We can offer you a month, fighting the strongest bulls in Spain.

BRENDA Bull-fighting? No, I don't want to do that.

TRAVEL AGENT Oh. Have you ever been to Paris?

MARTIN No, we haven't.

TRAVEL AGENT What about ten days in Paris? . . .

MARTIN That sounds marvellous!

TRAVEL AGENT . . . painting the outside of the Eiffel Tower.

BRENDA, MARTIN No, thanks!

TRAVEL AGENT Well, what about two weeks in Brighton?

BRENDA No, thanks!

MARTIN Just a minute. Did you say 'Brighton'?

TRAVEL AGENT Yes. How about two weeks in Brighton, staying in a nice quiet hotel by the sea?

BRENDA Well, yes . . .

MARTIN Yes, that sounds wonderful!

TRAVEL AGENT It's not very exciting. No camels, no snakes, but you can't have everything, can you?

BRENDA No. That's very nice. We'll take it.

MARTIN How much is it?

TRAVEL AGENT £50 each, please. Could you just sign this form for the reservations?

He gives Martin a form.

Just here, please.

Martin signs.

Thank you. And here. And here. And here. And . . . here. Thank you.

BRENDA Thank you very much.

MARTIN Goodbye.

TRAVEL AGENT Goodbye, and I hope you enjoy your holiday.

Martin and Brenda leave. The telephone rings.

(*On the telephone:*) Honest Harry's Happy Holidays. Can I help you? . . . Well, we've got some very nice holidays in Brighton, as a matter of fact . . .

Listening Comprehension

Questions

I 1 Why was the travel agent worried about his job?
II 2 Why did he say: 'It's a fish and chip shop'?
III 3 Why didn't Martin and Brenda want to go to Brighton?
4 Describe the holiday in the Sahara Desert.
5 How much did that holiday cost?
IV 6 Describe the holiday in the Arctic Ocean.
7 Why wasn't the map useful?
8 Martin said something was wrong with all the holidays. What?
V 9 Describe the holidays in Spain and France.
10 How much did Martin and Brenda pay for their holiday?

In answering Question 4, the students should mention as many of the details of the Sahara Desert holiday as possible, not necessarily trying to use exactly the same words as in the sketch itself, and they can of course add their own comments on the holiday ('Awful', 'Interesting' and so on qualify as descriptions!). This also applies to Questions 6 and 9. The full cost of the holiday in Question 5 is of course £805 (camels included).

Reading Comprehension

Read and Complete

Read this extract from the 'Honest Harry's Happy Holidays' brochure, and put in the missing words.

HOLIDAY NO. 247: THE SAHARA DESERT
45 days
£800 (£805 with stampede of camels)

Have you (1) . . . . . . visited the Sahara Desert? If not, this is the (2) . . . . . . for you. We can (3) . . . . . . you forty-five exciting days in the (4) . . . . . . of the Sahara Desert. You won't be bored (5) . . . . . . a moment, because there's always (6) . . . . . . to do. If you've (7) . . . . . . been in a sandstorm, don't miss this chance! There are (8) . . . . . . nearly every day. When you get home, you can (9) . . . . . . your friends all about the sandstorms you've (10) . . . . . . in – *and* about the (11) . . . . . . snakes you've seen. Holiday No. 247 is for (12) . . . . . . who want exciting holidays. If you are (13) . . . . . . of these people, this holiday is (14) . . . . . . you. It's certainly a holiday (15) . . . . . . remember!

The students can complete the text individually, in pairs or in groups, and their answers can be checked and discussed with the class as a whole. The missing words are: 1 ever, 2 holiday, 3 give/offer, 4 middle, 5 for, 6 plenty/something, 7 never, 8 sandstorms, 9 tell, 10 been, 11 dangerous, 12 people, 13 one, 14 for, 15 to/you'll/you'd.

Word Puzzle

Put the right words in the boxes.

	9	5	11	5	2	1
The Sahara is a	☐	☐	☐	☐	☐	☐

	11	1	3	13	–	5	9	5	
The	☐	☐	☐	☐	☐	☐	☐	☐	of camels cost £5 extra.

	7	2	14	–	12	1	8	10
Martin and Brenda finally chose a holiday in	☐	☐	☐	☐	☐	☐	☐	☐

Now fill these boxes with the right letters:

1 2 3 4 5 6   7 2 8 3 9 5 10 11   1 12 5   13 14 10 9

☐☐☐☐☐☐   ☐☐☐☐☐☐☐☐   ☐☐☐   ☐☐☐☐

There are two letters missing. Can you guess them? Can you say what the expression means?

Solution: The Sahara is a *desert*. The *stampede* of camels cost £5 extra. Martin and Brenda finally chose a holiday in *Brighton*. Thus, when the boxes are filled, the result is: TRA–E– BROADENS THE MIND. The missing letters are V and L, completing the popular saying about one of the benefits of travel.

Communicating

1 *Making Suggestions*

In the sketch, the travel agent made several suggestions about holidays:

How about the Sahara Desert?
How about the Arctic Ocean?
What about ten days in Paris?
What about two weeks in Brighton?

In pairs, practice asking for suggestions and making suggestions about birthday presents, for example:

What should I buy for	my mother? my uncle? Bernard?	→	How about What about	a . . . . ? some . . . . ?	→

That's a good idea.
No, I don't think so.

Make suggestions for an evening out:

What shall we do this evening?	→	How about What about	going to the cinema? visiting Bob?

2 Polite Requests for Information

In the sketch, Brenda said 'We'd like some information about holidays'.
Practise asking for information about these things:

holidays in Scotland/stereo equipment/central heating

Make dialogues like this:

– Good morning. I wonder if you can help me. I'd like some information about . . . . – Certainly, sir/madam. What sort of . . . . . . are you interested in? – Well, something that's not too expensive. – I see.

Exercise 1: Point out that 'How about . . .?' and 'What about . . .?' are informal ways of making suggestions. The first pair-practice is based on the pattern 'How/What about' + noun, the second on 'How/What about' + '-ing'. After practising these two patterns, the students could make suggestions for showing a visitor around the town: a question like 'Where shall I take him/her?' can elicit both patterns ('How about the cathedral?' or 'How about taking him to the zoo?' etc.).
Exercise 2: The dialogues can be practised simply as controlled substitutions, using the subjects provided, or the students can use the four lines as a starting-point and continue with more questions and answers of their own.

In Your Own Words

Re-enact the sketch in your own words, without reading from the text. Do it in short sections. These words will remind you:

It is useful, when re-enacting this sketch, for the 'travel agent' to sit behind a desk, with two chairs beside it for the 'customers'. A few 'brochures' on the desk (real ones can of course be used, but if none are available, sheets of paper can represent them) will give the 'travel agent' something to refer to as he/she mentions the different holidays. A sheet of paper for the form which Martin signs is also useful. The telephone can be mimed, or a plastic toy telephone can be used.

Further Role-playing Activities

1 Suggesting and Persuading

The students can improvise dialogues similar to that between the travel agent and the customers in the sketch. The improvisations can be done in pairs (travel agent and customer) or in threes (travel agent and two customers). Prepare cue-cards for the students. For example:

TRAVEL AGENT	CUSTOMER
You are a travel agent. You have to sell holidays on the moon.	You are a customer. You want a holiday in Scotland. Do not accept any other holiday.

The 'travel agent' should try as hard as possible to persuade the 'customers' to take the holiday he suggests, and the 'customers' should insist on the holiday they want.
A variation on this is to give the 'customers' more specific roles (e.g. an elderly professor, a young couple who like water-skiing, etc.), so that the 'travel agent' finally has to suggest something suitable.

2 *'Presenting the Facts'*
The students should work in groups and 'present the facts' about their town, making it sound as attractive as possible.
In a multi-national class the students should imagine that they are travel agents presenting the facts about their own town, village or city. In answer to questions such as 'What's it like in . . . ?' and 'Is there anything to do?' they should give relevant facts ('There's a . . .', 'There are several . . .', 'Oh, yes, there's plenty to do. . . .' and so on).

Pronunciation Practice

1 *Stress*
Play the final part of section III of the sketch again, and draw the students' attention particularly to these two lines:

– Is it exciting?
– Exc*i*ting? It's *ter*rifying!

After practising this exchange, the students can use these pairs of words to make others:

difficult → impossible	big → enormous
good → fantastic	small → tiny
clever → brilliant	interesting → fascinating

After practising the questions and answers, the students can say what they think is being referred to in each one. For example, the first exchange ('Is it difficult?', 'Difficult? It's impossible!') could refer to a crossword puzzle, reading someone's handwriting, tying a complicated knot, etc. Alternatively, the students can be given only the first word in each pair, and work out what the appropriate 'heightened' word for the response would be.

2 *Consonants*
In the name of the travel agency in the sketch, the sound /h/ occurs at the beginning of three words: '*H*arry's *H*appy *H*olidays'. The students could invent similar alliterative names for other shops and businesses. For example:

a butcher's shop	:	Martin's Marvellous Meat
a baker's	:	Bernard's Better Bread
a greengrocer's	:	Fred's Fantastic Fruit
a car showroom	:	Colin's (or: Kevin's) Classic Car Company

Writing

An Extract from a Brochure

Look at the extract from the brochure ('Read and Complete', p. 114). Choose one of the other holidays:

- the Arctic Ocean
- the Amazon Jungle
- Spain
- Paris
- Brighton

and write a similar advertisement for it.

The students should set out their extract from the brochure in the same way as the 'Read and Complete' text, i.e. the number, name, length and cost of the holiday, followed by details of its advantages. They can include information from the sketch, and add their own ideas; they can also use expressions each as 'This is the holiday for you' or 'A holiday to remember', which the travel agent himself used. Instead of choosing one of the holidays mentioned in the sketch, they can of course choose another part of the world, their own country, or indeed somewhere farther afield such as Mars.

What Do You Think?

Travel

A What is the worst holiday you've ever had? What is the best holiday you've ever had? Why was the bad one bad and the good one good?

B If you had one year, and all the money you needed, what would be your perfect holiday? Plan a trip, starting in your town and lasting for one year.

The first topic is designed for conversation practice in groups: individuals in the groups first recount the worst holiday they have ever had, using anecdotes of what happened to show why they didn't enjoy it. Other students can ask them to clarify, give more details, and so on. The students can then discuss enjoyable experiences they have had on holidays. For the second topic, the students can also work in groups, or better, in pairs, and decide on an itinerary. They can make a list of the places they would visit, or put them into a diagram or stylised map, and after their work in pairs or groups, explain their itinerary and their reasons for choosing it to the rest of the class. Either of these activities could be followed up with written work.

13

Gerry Brown's Driving Test

This sketch was first performed in July 1976. On stage, the car is represented by four chairs, and everything is done in mime: the climbing in and out of the car, the driving along, turning, stopping and so on, accompanied by vocal noises for the engine. The script has been slightly altered here: in the stage version, the examiner falls for Gerry at the end and he passes his test; and there is a great deal of confusion over seating in the car, which has also been omitted.

This sketch is suitable for Intermediate and more Advanced students because of the variety of different structural patterns.

Attitudes and Functions

Reassurance
Now don't worry. I've flown aeroplanes, you know.

Gratitude
It's very good of you to lend me your car.
– Oh, that's all right, Gerry.

Giving Instructions
I'd like you to drive the car straight down the road.
Turn right, Mr Brown.

Giving Advice
Now listen, Gerry. There's only one way you can pass this test . . . Be polite.

Telling Someone Where They Went Wrong
You should have brought your *own* glasses.
You should have turned *right*.

Formal, Polite Offers
Allow me to open the door for you.

Structure and Usage

Main Point
'Should(n't) have' and Past Participle
e.g. You should have brought your *own* glasses.
I should have stayed in bed today.

Other Points
Present Perfect and Past Simple tenses
e.g. I've flown aeroplanes, you know.
My uncle has worn these for 25 years.
You have had driving lessons, haven't you?
– Yes. I had one last night.
Reported Speech
e.g. You told the authorities that your eyes were perfect.
He says they're marvellous.
Future Simple for Immediate Decision
e.g. I'll put them on.
I think I'll come with you, just in case.

Note the Following Words and Expressions
the big day more or less the same Up she goes! not exactly perfect brain surgeon examiner just in case traffic lights

Suggested Preliminary Practice
Practise 'should(n't) have . . .' as used for 'telling someone where they went wrong'. You could use one or more of these situations for prompting students' comments in the form: 'You should(n't) have . . .'

1 Say that you have just returned from a holiday, and got badly sunburnt while you were away.
2 Say that someone grabbed your bag and ran off with it, but you didn't do anything.
3 Say that you bought a clock, and that when you took it home, it didn't work so you threw it away.

The students can make comments, such as:

You should have used some sun-tan lotion. You shouldn't have stayed in the sun so much.
You should have shouted 'Stop. thief!' You should have told the police.
You shouldn't have bought it without checking it first. You should have taken it back to the shop.

Preliminary Questions
1 Why did Gerry Brown's friend meet him before his driving test?
2 Do you think Gerry was ready for his driving test?
3 Did he pass?

13

Gerry Brown's Driving Test

SCENE	A car
CHARACTERS	Gerry Brown Brian Smith, Gerry's friend A driving examiner

I

Brian has just arrived at the test centre in his car. He is sitting in it, waiting for Gerry.

BRIAN Hmm. . . . Three o'clock. Where is he? . . . Ah, there he is. Gerry! Gerry!

Gerry comes to the car.

GERRY Ah, hello!

BRIAN Hello, Gerry.

Brian gets out of the car.

Well, the big day, eh?

GERRY Yes, my driving test. It's very good of you to lend me your car.

BRIAN Oh, that's all right, Gerry. You *have* had driving lessons, haven't you?

GERRY Oh, yes. Well . . . I had *one*.

BRIAN One?

GERRY Yes. I had one last night. It was very good.

BRIAN One last night! That's not enough. You should have had at least *ten*!

GERRY Now don't worry. I've flown aeroplanes, you know, and it's all more or less the same. You just jump in, switch on, and up she goes!

BRIAN Yes, but this isn't an *aeroplane*. It's a *car*. *My* car!

GERRY Oh yes, I can see that.

II BRIAN Hmm . . . *that's* another problem.

GERRY What?

BRIAN Your eyes.

GERRY What's the matter with my eyes?

BRIAN Well, they're not exactly perfect, are they?

GERRY Well, I know I can't see very well, but –

BRIAN But you told the authorities that your eyes were perfect. You shouldn't have done that.

GERRY Yes, I know. But don't worry, everything will be all right. I borrowed these glasses from my uncle, and he says they're marvellous.

BRIAN Your *uncle's* glasses! But Gerry, you should have brought your *own* glasses.

GERRY I haven't got any of my own. But don't worry, my uncle has worn these for twenty-five years, and he's a brain surgeon.

BRIAN Gerry –

GERRY Look, I'll put them on.

He puts on the glasses.

There. Oh. . . . Um . . . Brian? . . . Brian?

He bumps into the car.

Oh!

III BRIAN Gerry, look, here comes the examiner.

GERRY Oh yes, I see. He looks like a very nice man.

BRIAN Gerry, it's not a *man*. It's a *woman*.

GERRY Oh.

BRIAN Now listen, Gerry. There's only one way you can pass this test.

GERRY Yes?

BRIAN Be polite.

GERRY Be polite?

BRIAN Yes. Be *very very* polite . . . and remember: Always open the door for a lady.

GERRY Be polite, and open the door for a lady. Be polite and –

BRIAN Shh, Gerry. Here she is.

The examiner arrives.

EXAMINER Mr Brown?

GERRY Er . . . yes.

EXAMINER I'm the examiner. Shall we get in?

GERRY Er . . . yes. Allow me to open the door for you.

He opens the door and the examiner gets into the car.

EXAMINER Thank you.

He closes the door.

GERRY Was that all right?

BRIAN Very good, Gerry. But I think I'll come with you, just in case.

GERRY All right.

Gerry and Brian get into the car. Brian sits in the back.

IV EXAMINER Now, Mr Brown. I'd like you to drive the car straight down the road.

GERRY Straight down the road, yes.

He tries to drive away. The car stalls.

Oh. Sorry.

He tries again, and drives away very fast.

EXAMINER Turn right, Mr Brown.

Gerry turns left.

BRIAN Gerry! You turned *left*. She said 'Right'. You should have turned *right*.

GERRY (*Cheerfully:*) Sorry.

EXAMINER Turn left, Mr Brown.

Gerry turns right.

BRIAN Gerry! You turned *right*. You should have turned *left*.

EXAMINER The traffic lights are red, Mr Brown.

BRIAN }
EXAMINER } Red!

Gerry stops the car at the traffic lights.

GERRY Ha, ha! Very good, eh? Straight on?

EXAMINER Er . . . n-n-no, Mr Brown. I think I'll get out here.

GERRY Oh. Allow me to open the door for you.

EXAMINER No, no, thank you. That won't be necessary.

She gets out of the car and walks away.

I should have stayed in bed today. I knew it . . . I knew it was going to be a bad day.

GERRY Oh, dear.

BRIAN I told you you should have had more lessons, Gerry.

GERRY Ah, green!

Gerry drives away very fast.

BRIAN Gerry! Gerry! Slow down, Gerry! Gerry!!

Listening Comprehension

Questions

I 1 Was Gerry confident about his driving test?
2 Why was Brian nervous about Gerry's driving?
II 3 Had Gerry lied to anyone?
4 Were the glasses useful to Gerry?
III 5 What advice did Brian give Gerry?
6 Did Gerry follow his advice?
7 Why did Brian get into the car, too?
IV 8 How many mistakes did Gerry make?
9 Who was the calmest person in the car?
10 Why did the examiner get out of the car?

In answering Questions 1, 2 and 9, which concern the feelings of the characters, the students should support their answers by referring to what the characters said, or to the way they spoke. Also note that in answer to Question 2, there are two reasons for Brian's nervousness in section I (Gerry's inexperience, and the fact that he was going to drive Brian's car), and a third reason in section II (Gerry's eyesight). Question 4 is debatable: Gerry couldn't see very well with the glasses, but possibly his eyesight was even worse without them!

Reading Comprehension

Read and Complete

The text below is taken from the British 'Highway Code'. Read it and put in the missing words.

Keep your vehicle (1) . . . . . good condition. Pay particular attention (2) . . . . . lights, brakes and tyres.
Do not (3) . . . . . a journey if you (4) . . . . . tired. Never drive (5) . . . . . drinking alcohol.
Do (6) . . . . . drive if you (7) . . . . . unwell.
If you (8) . . . . . spectacles, wear them.
Use your (9) . . . . . often, so that you can see what is behind you.
Driving (10) . . . . . long distances may make you feel (11) . . . . . Make sure there is plenty of fresh (12) . . . . . in your vehicle. If you become tired (13) . . . . . a journey, stop and rest at a suitable parking place. You (14) . . . . . obey the speed limits for the road and (15) . . . . . your vehicle. Any speed limit is a maximum. It does (16) . . . . . mean that it is safe to (17) . . . . . at that speed.
Go much more (18) . . . . . if the road is wet (19) . . . . . icy, or if (20) . . . . . is fog.

The missing words are: 1 in 2 to 3 start/begin 4 are/feel/are feeling 5 after 6 not 7 are/feel/are feeling 8 need 9 mirror 10 for 11 sleepy/tired 12 air 13 on/during 14 must 15 for 16 not 17 drive 18 slowly 19 or 20 there.

The students can complete the text individually, in pairs or in groups. After their answers have been checked and discussed, the text can be used as a basis for some oral practice, with questions initially from the teacher, and then from the students, working in pairs. A useful pattern for the question is:

What should you remember about	alcohol? spectacles? the mirror? long distances? bad weather?

Word Puzzle

Put the correct words in the horizontal lines.

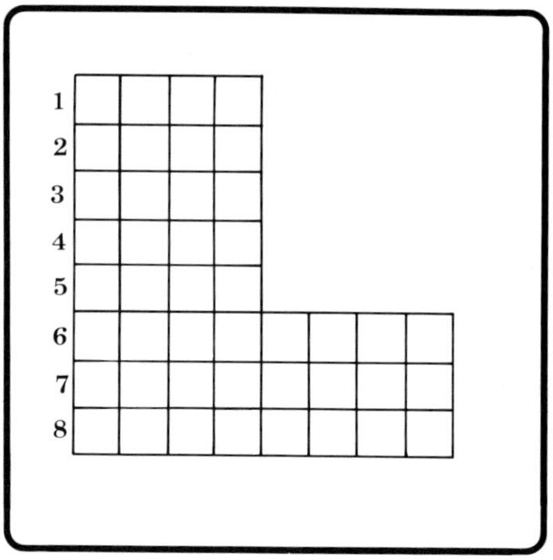

1 Gerry should . . . . . had more than one lesson.
2 Gerry's . . . . . weren't exactly perfect.

3  This sign means: Turn . . . . .

4 Gerry did not . . . . . his test.
5 When Gerry drove too fast, Brian told him to slow . . . . .
6 Gerry had two . . . . . : he couldn't drive properly, and his eyesight was bad.
7 The glasses weren't Gerry's. He had . . . . . them from his uncle.
8 Gerry was very polite to the . . . . ., but it didn't do any good.

When you have filled in all the words, look at the first letters of Nos. 1–4. They should spell a word, one which Brian might have shouted at the end of the sketch.

Solution: 1 have 2 eyes 3 left 4 pass 5 down 6 problems 7 borrowed 8 examiner. The first letters of Nos. 1–4 spell 'Help!'.

Communicating

1 Thanking Someone for a Favour

Look at these lines from the sketch:

Gerry	:	It's very good of you to lend me your car.
Brian	:	Oh, that's all right, Gerry.

Think of your own examples, and practice in pairs:

It's It was	very	good nice	of you to	That's all right. Don't mention it. It's/It was a pleasure. Not at all.

2 Giving Advice

In the sketch, Brian gave Gerry some advice. He said: 'There's only one way you can pass this test. . . . Be very very polite. . . . and always open the door for a lady.'
In pairs, make short dialogues. In each pair, Student A says what his/her problem is, and asks for advice. Here are some problems:

– My sister is very very angry.
– I've got hiccups.
– I've had a terrible cough for months.

Student B gives some advice, using the expression:

'There's only one way you can (calm her down). . . . .
(get rid of them). . . . .
(get rid of that cough) . . . .'

Exercise 1: Note that the four possible responses differ in their level of formality: 'That's all right' is the most casual, and 'Not at all' the most formal. In practising in pairs, the students can, of course, invent unlikely favours for which they are saying Thank you, for example: 'It was very nice of you to give me your Rolls-Royce.'
* **Exercise 2:** After practising with one partner, the students could move on to another. This will put them in contact with several different pieces of advice, making the opening phrase 'There's only one way you can . . .' rather ironic.

In Your Own Words

Re-enact the sketch in your own words, without reading from the text. Do it in short sections. These words will remind you:

If possible, for the re-enacting of this sketch, arrange four chairs to represent the car. Encourage the students to use plenty of mime and gestures: getting into and out of the car, opening and closing the doors, stopping and starting, etc. Useful simple 'props' are a pair of glasses for 'Gerry', and a pen and a few large sheets of paper clipped together for the 'examiner'. The students may like to change the ending of the sketch, for example, they may like to make the examiner give Gerry a pass certificate in order to escape.

Further Role-playing Activities

1 Reading Letters and Numbers Aloud

This is a simple skill, but one which often proves a challenge even to good students (see also *The Ticket Inspector*, 'Communicating' 2, on p. 13). It can be practised by two very simple activities:

1 *A driving examiner and a candidate*
In a driving test, the examiner asks the candidate to read a car number-plate. Put several 'number-plates' on the blackboard, and take the role of the examiner, asking the students to read them aloud. (The 'number-plates' can be in British or local style.)

2 *An optician and a customer*
Bring a large optician's letter-chart into the classroom, and ask the students to read from it, either a string of letters, or individual letters at random. Then let the students take the role of the optician, and point to the letters to be read.

2 A Driving Lesson

Students in pairs (with at least one in each pair who can drive!) can improvise a driving lesson. Place two chairs side by side, to represent the front seats of a car. One student takes the role of the instructor, and the other that of the learner-driver. The instructor should give clear instructions on how to start up and drive off. The learner-driver should follow the instructions in mime, and ask for explanations of any instructions which are unclear. Before doing this exercise check that the students know the relevant car vocabulary, e.g. clutch, gears, brakes, accelerator, etc.

Pronunciation Practice

Stress to Make Contrasts Clear

Play the first section of the sketch to the students again. Point out the stress used to contrast 'ten' with 'one' in these sentences:

Gerry : Well . . . I had *one*.

Brian : You should have had at least *ten*!

Then play the rest of the sketch, asking the students to find five other examples of stress used in this way. The five examples are:

1 This isn't an *aeroplane*. It's a *car*.
2 You *uncle's* glasses! But Gerry, you should have brought your *own* glasses.
3 Gerry, it's not a *man*. It's a *woman*.
4 Gerry! You turned *left*. She said 'Right'. You should have turned *right*.
5 Gerry! You turned *right*. You should have turned *left.*

Writing

Notes for a Report

These are the examiner's notes about Gerry's test:

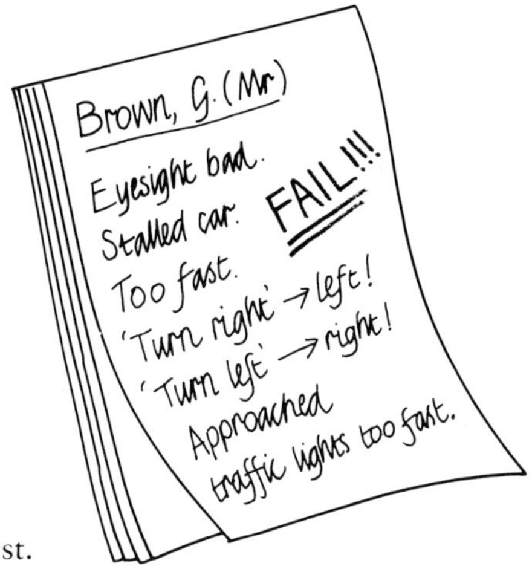

Use the notes to write the examiner's report on the test.

With the class as a whole, discuss suggestions for turning the notes into full sentences. The students can then write the report as a pair or group activity in class, or for homework.

What Do You Think?

Tests and Examinations

Some people love tests and examinations. Most people don't like them very much. Do you dislike them? Why? What tests and examinations have you taken? Are tests and examinations necessary?

* In groups the students can first discuss tests and examinations they have taken, either school exams or practical tests. They can say whether they like or dislike them, and give their reasons. Then, from the examples they have given, they can say which tests and examinations they think are necessary and which are unnecessary.

14
Giovanni's Café

This sketch was first performed in 1975. The stage version consisted of two sketches, one set in Paris, with only Geoffrey and Dorothy, and a second (coming later on in the show) set in Rome, and involving all four characters. The version here is a combination of elements from both these sketches. The idea for the sketch came from the thought that there are a lot of humorous possibilities in the situation where two people who want to be alone, for example at a café table, are interrupted by a third.
This sketch is suitable for Intermediate and more Advanced students.

Attitudes and Functions
Asking for Clarification
What exactly do you mean by 'young and innocent'?
What – at the college?
'Green'. What do you mean?
What's he talking about?

Meeting and Introducing
Teresa, this is my wife, Dorothy.
– Delighted to meet you.

Polite Requests
May I sit here?

Surprise
Just a minute – it's Geoffrey – Geoffrey Burton!
– Good God! Teresa Pilkington!
Goodness me! Look at that magnificent telephone-box!

Structure and Usage
Main Point
'So'/'so much'/'such a . . .'
e.g. His life was so boring.
We've got so much to talk about.
It's such a beautiful day.

Other Points
Present Perfect tense, with 'since'/'for'
e.g. I've known Geoffrey for years and years – since we were both young and innocent.

Reported Speech
e.g. You told me you loved that college in the mountains.

Note the Following Words and Expressions
romantic innocent remarkable magnificent honest statue kindergarten delighted (to meet you) a second honeymoon all the time in the world hated every minute of it

Suggested Preliminary Practice
In the sketch, 'so' and 'such' are used for intensification only ('His life was so boring', 'It's so nice, sitting here with you.' etc.), and not in the pattern ' . . . so/such a . . . that . . .'. Preliminary practice might therefore focus on this simple but useful intensification usage.
Straightforward prompts and responses can be used, e.g.

. . . is a good book, . . . is a good film, The . . . is a good car, The . . . is a good restaurant	isn't it?

Yes, but it's so	long. long. expensive. expensive.

Take the opportunity to point out the differences between 'so' and 'too'. If the speaker had used 'too' instead of 'so' in the answer this would have been a more categorical response, for example: 'The . . . is a good restaurant, isn't it?' 'Yes, but it's too expensive. We'll have to go somewhere else.'

Preliminary Questions
1 Why were Geoffrey and Dorothy Burton in Rome?
2 Was Geoffrey pleased to see Teresa Pilkington?
3 Had Geoffrey met the waiter before?

14
Giovanni's Café

SCENE	A pavement café in Rome
CHARACTERS	Geoffrey Burton Dorothy Burton, his wife Teresa Pilkington Giovanni

I

Geoffrey and Dorothy are sitting at a table in the café.

GEOFFREY Well, here we are in Rome. The sun is shining, and we haven't got a care in the world.

DOROTHY Yes, Rome is *so* beautiful.

GEOFFREY And it's such a beautiful day.

DOROTHY This square looks lovely in the sunshine.

GEOFFREY And it's so nice, sitting here with you. No trains to catch . . .

DOROTHY No telephones to answer . . .

GEOFFREY No boring business people to talk to . . . Do you know, this is the first holiday we've had for five years – since we were married.

DOROTHY And it's our first visit to Rome, too. It's like a second honeymoon.

GEOFFREY Yes, and now we're alone together, with all the time in the world.

DOROTHY Yes.

GEOFFREY Just you, and me, and romantic Rome.

DOROTHY Yes.

II *Teresa comes to their table.*

TERESA Excuse me, do you speak English?

GEOFFREY Yes.

TERESA May I sit here?

GEOFFREY Er . . . oh . . . yes.

Teresa sits down.

TERESA Thank you. Just a minute – it's Geoffrey – Geoffrey Burton!

GEOFFREY Good God! Teresa Pilkington!

TERESA Geoffrey, darling! How lovely to see you! It's been so long since we –

GEOFFREY Er . . . Teresa, this is my *wife*, Dorothy.

TERESA Oh, your wife. Delighted to meet you.

DOROTHY So you know Geoffrey, do you?

TERESA Oh yes, Geoffrey and I are old friends, aren't we, Geoffrey?

GEOFFREY No. Er . . . yes. Er . . . what are you doing in Rome, Teresa?

DOROTHY You're old friends, are you?

TERESA Oh yes, I've known Geoffrey for years and years, since we were both young and innocent.

GEOFFREY Goodness me! Look at that remarkable statue!

DOROTHY Geoffrey! . . . Tell me, Miss Pilkington, what exactly do you mean by 'young and innocent'?

TERESA Well, darling, before Geoffrey met me, he was just an innocent boy.

GEOFFREY Er . . . yes . . . we met at kindergarten.

TERESA Geoffrey, you know that's not what I mean.

DOROTHY Well, what exactly *do* you mean?

GEOFFREY Good Lord! Look at that magnificent telephone-box!

DOROTHY Geoffrey!

GEOFFREY Well, you don't see telephone-boxes like that in England, do you?

III TERESA Poor Geoffrey! Before he met me, his life was so boring. He was a student at an awful college in the mountains, and he hated every minute of it.

DOROTHY But Geoffrey – you told me you *loved* that college in the mountains!

TERESA Ah yes, that's because he met *me* there.

DOROTHY What – at the college?

TERESA No, in the mountains.

GEOFFREY Er, Dorothy, I think we'd better go. The Colosseum closes at six o'clock, you know.

DOROTHY Sit down, Geoffrey. It's only half past eleven.

TERESA Yes, I remember that day so well – the day that we met. The mountains were so beautiful, the sky was so blue –

DOROTHY – and Geoffrey was so *green*, I suppose.

TERESA 'Green'? What do you mean?

DOROTHY 'Green'. Young and innocent. Just the way you like them, I suppose.

TERESA Well, really!

Teresa gets up.

Excuse me! . . . Goodbye, Geoffrey. (*Sarcastically:*) Delighted to have met you, Mrs Burton.

GEOFFREY Teresa . . . um . . .

TERESA Goodbye, Geoffrey.

Teresa leaves.

IV GEOFFREY Oh, dear.

DOROTHY So before you met her, you were just an innocent boy! You told me I was the first woman in your life, and I believed you . . . and *I've* been *so* honest with *you*.

GEOFFREY Yes, Dorothy.

DOROTHY I've told you everything.

GEOFFREY Yes, Dorothy, I know. I was the first man in your life.

DOROTHY The first and *only* man, Geoffrey.

Giovanni comes to the table.

GEOFFREY Oh . . . waiter. I'll have a Martini, please.

GIOVANNI Certainly, sir. And for you, madam? Oh! Dorothy!

DOROTHY Giovanni!

GIOVANNI Dorothy!

GEOFFREY Giovanni?

GIOVANNI Dorothy, it's wonderful to see you again!

GEOFFREY Dorothy, have you met this man before?

DOROTHY Well, Geoffrey –

GIOVANNI Dorothy, it must be five years!

DOROTHY Six, Giovanni, six!

GIOVANNI And now you've come back to Rome!

GEOFFREY Come back? What's he talking about?

DOROTHY Well, Geoffrey –

GIOVANNI Come with me, Dorothy. We've got *so* much to talk about!

DOROTHY Oh . . . er, yes . . . um . . . excuse me, Geoffrey.

Giovanni and Dorothy leave.

GEOFFREY Dorothy! Dorothy! Dorothy!

Listening Comprehension

Questions

I 1 Where were Geoffrey and Dorothy sitting?
2 Had they been to Rome before?
II 3 Did Dorothy know Teresa?
4 Did Dorothy like Teresa?
5 Why did Geoffrey say 'Look at that remarkable statue!'?
III 6 Where did Geoffrey first meet Teresa?
7 Why did Teresa get up and leave?
IV 8 Dorothy said: 'I've told you everything.' Was this true?
9 Was Dorothy surprised to see Giovanni?
10 How did Geoffrey feel at the end?

Question 2 may lead to some discussion: Geoffrey and Dorothy had not been to Rome together before (Dorothy said: 'It's our first visit to Rome'), but – as becomes clear in section 4 – Dorothy had been to Rome before (Giovanni said: 'Now you've come back to Rome!'); it is not clear from the sketch whether Geoffrey had been to Rome before. In answering Question 4, the students should say *why* Dorothy did not like Teresa.

Reading Comprehension

Read and Complete

This is a postcard which Geoffrey and Dorothy sent from Rome to a friend in London. (They posted it before they met Teresa and Giovanni.) Read it and put in the missing words.

> August 17th
>
> Dear Sandra,
>
> Here we are in Rome. We've been here ①.... three days, and we've ②.... very lucky with the weather. The sun's been ③.... non-stop, and all the squares and fountains ④.... very beautiful in the sunshine. It's so ⑤...., being away from London, with no trains to ⑥.... and no ⑦.... to answer. The city is full ⑧.... tourists - perhaps we'll meet ⑨.... we know!
>
> Wish you were with us - Rome is ⑩.... a beautiful city!
>
> Dorothy & Geoffrey

The students can complete the text individually, in pairs or in groups, and their answers can be checked and discussed with the class as a whole. The missing words are: 1 for 2 been 3 shining 4 look/are 5 nice 6 catch 7 telephones 8 of 9 someone 10 such/really/certainly. Point out, if necessary, that 'Wish you were with us' is shortened from 'We wish you were with us' (and that 'Wish you were here' is a 'postcard cliché' in English).

Word Puzzle

All the answers in this puzzle are adjectives. They were all used in the sketch. When you have filled in all the words, the letters in the vertical box should all be the same.

1 This described Rome and the weather.
2 This described the statue.
3 This described the telephone-box.
4 This described the sky.
5 This described Geoffrey.
6 No. 5 meant 'young and . . . .'
7 'How . . . . to see you!'
8 '. . . . . to meet you.'
9 'It's . . . . to see you again.'
10 Dorothy said she had been . . . . with Geoffrey.

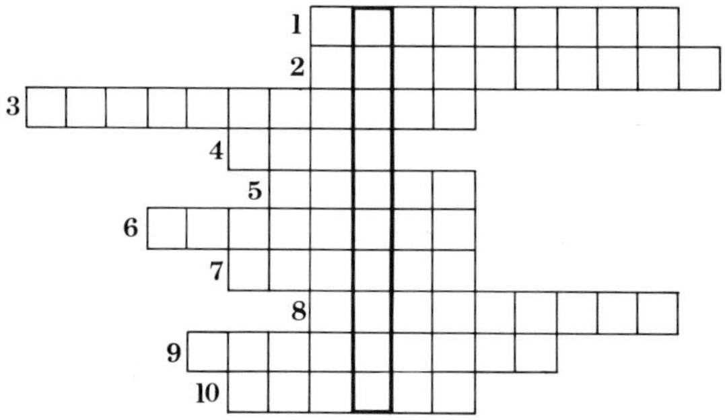

Solution: 1 beautiful 2 remarkable 3 magnificent 4 blue 5 green 6 innocent 7 lovely 8 delighted 9 wonderful 10 honest. The letters in the vertical box are all 'E'.

Communicating

1 *Asking for Clarification*

In the sketch, Dorothy asked Teresa: 'What exactly do you mean by "young and innocent"?'

Later, Teresa asked Dorothy: '"Green"? What do you mean?'

Use these ideas to practice asking for clarification:

Smoking is *bad for you.* Hard work is *a good thing.* Watching TV is *a waste of time.*	What exactly do you mean by '. . .'? '. . .' What do you mean?

2 *Leaving Someone You've Just Met*

When Teresa left, she said: 'Delighted to have met you.' This is a formal expression. You can also use these less formal expressions:

(It was) (very)	nice meeting you. nice to meet you.

In threes, practise like this:

A introduces B and C, and leaves them.
B and C ask each other about their jobs.
B then leaves C (e.g. to speak to someone else).

Exercise 1: In using the ideas, the first speaker should respond to the request for clarification, for example by saying: 'Well, it's bad for your health – it may shorten your life . . .', 'Well, it's better than doing nothing . . .' or 'Well, most of the programmes are boring . . .'. The second speaker can then agree or disagree, and a brief improvised conversation can ensue.

Exercise 2: See 'Further Role-Playing Activities' (A) on p. 22, for a short model dialogue on Meeting and Introducing People. Before student B leaves student C, he could say, for example, 'Excuse me, I must go and say "Hello" to X'.

In Your Own Words

Re-enact the sketch in your own words, without reading from the text. Do it in short sections. These words will remind you:

I
beautiful
holiday
alone together

II
Geoffrey Burton!
my wife
old friends
young and innocent

III
college
mountains
green
Goodbye

IV
honest
first man
waiter
Dorothy!

For re-enacting this sketch, a table with three chairs at it is all that is required. For a more elaborate 'performance', 'props' and costumes as follows are useful: a bright tablecloth and miscellaneous objects for the table (e.g. a menu, salt and pepper or sugar containers), sun-glasses and possibly a camera for the visitors to Rome, an apron or short jacket and a tray for Giovanni. 'Geoffrey' and 'Dorothy' should begin sitting close together – Teresa's arrival interrupts their romantic moment.

Further Role-playing Activities

1 Surprise Meetings

This activity should be done in groups of three, and consists of improvising conversations in a situation parallel to the sketch. Give the students cue-cards with information about their roles. For example:

THE COUPLE	THE THIRD PERSON
You are an engaged couple. You are on holiday in Paris. Your names are Tom Johnson and Alice Brown. Alice used to know Brian Williams at school.	Your name is Brian Williams. You are an engineer. You are on holiday in Paris. You used to know Alice Brown at school.
or:	
You are a grandmother and grandson. You are on holiday in Athens. Your names are Martha and Jack Green. Martha used to work with Diana Walker.	Your name is Diana Walker. You are a retired teacher. You are on holiday in Athens. You used to work with Martha Green.

The couple should begin, sitting at a café table, or a table in a hotel restaurant, etc. and the third person should join them at the table. The two people then recognize each other, and introductions take place followed by questions about reasons for being in Paris/Athens/etc.

2 Joining in a Conversation

This is another activity for groups of three. In this activity, the 'third person' should imagine that he/she is visiting a café in his/her own town. He/She joins two people at a table, hears that they are talking in English, and joins in their conversation ('Excuse me, are you English?'), asking them about their impressions of the town and recommending places they should visit.

Pronunciation Practice

A Question-Tags

Most Question-tags are Positive if the statement is Negative, and vice-versa. If the voice falls on the tag, confirmation is expected, and if the voice rises on the tag, the speaker is less sure that confirmation will be forthcoming. Most courses give practice with these types of Question-tags. There is another type, in which *both* the statement and the tag are Positive, with the voice *rising* on the tag. There are two examples in section II of the sketch:

– So you know Geoffrey, do you? / You're old friends, are you?

This type of tag is often used when the speaker has deduced something from the situation, and, as in these examples, the speaker may be using a sarcastic tone of voice. Play the examples to the students and draw their attention to the intonation and the attitude. They can then practise and discuss similar examples:

1 You think you deserve more money, do you?
2 He wants to marry you, does he?
3 It's the best car on the market, is it?

B Surprise

Play the sketch to the students again and ask them to find as many examples of surprise as they can. There are quite a number, for example:

– Just a minute – it's Geoffrey – Geoffrey Burton!   Good God! Teresa Pilkington! etc.

They can include in the examples the occasions where Geoffrey feigns surprise in order to change the subject. For example: Goodness me! Look at that remarkable statue!

Writing

A Postcard

Look at the postcard which Dorothy and Geoffrey wrote from Rome (p. 131). Imagine you are on holiday (choose a place), and write a similar postcard to a friend.
Say how long you've been there, what the weather is like, what you've seen, and how long you're going to stay. Add any other ideas you like.

This exercise can be done individually for homework, or in pairs in class. The students can model their postcard very closely on Dorothy and Geoffrey's ('Here we are/I am in . . . We've/I've been here for . . . The weather . . . It's so nice . . . The city is . . . Wish you were here . . .') or they can use their own ideas in a less controlled way. They can 'address' their cards to other students in the class, who can then read them and comment on anything they don't understand, or on any mistakes in the English.

What Do You Think?

Tourists

In the holiday season, tourists are everywhere: there are crowds of them on beautiful beaches, in pleasant little villages, on mountainsides, in city streets. Do tourists *spoil* these places? If your town council decided to ban tourists, what would you say?
Is it better to be a tourist in a large group, or a 'solo traveller'?

The students can discuss this topic in groups. They can first discuss the advantages and disadvantages of tourism, with one member of the group listing the points made. The class as a whole can then compare their findings. The students can then continue their discussion in groups with the subsidiary topic (travelling in large groups vs. travelling alone), giving their personal preferences and reasons.

15

Shakespeare's House

This sketch was first performed in July 1974. (The idea came from an example used by one of the ETT members in a structure-practice lesson.) We have adapted it slightly for this book, but the 'plot' remains the same as the stage-version. We were originally going to include more quotations from Shakespeare, but in the end stuck to just the most well-known one of all.
This sketch is suitable for more Advanced students.

Attitudes and Functions
Making Deductions
You must be Shakespeare's grandson.
That must be Shakespeare's typewriter.
He must have written all his plays on this.

Taking Leave
I hope we haven't disturbed you too much.

Surprise
What? Eh? What's going on? Tourists?

'Puzzlement'
Interesting? Living here?
What are you talking about?

Irritation
Don't be silly!
No, of course he didn't.

Excitement
Sidney, look!
Ethel! Look at this!

Structure and Usage
Main Point
'must be . . .'/'can't be . . .'
'must have (been) . . .'/'can't have (been) . . .'
e.g. This must be Shakespeare's television.
He can't have been comfortable, sitting there.

Other Points
Past Simple tense
e.g. He probably sat at this table.
Shakespeare didn't use a typewriter.

Note the Following Words and Expressions
tragedy (play) typewriter microphone ashtray grandson souvenir disturb There must be some mistake.
'To be, or not to be – that is the question.' from *Hamlet*, Act III, Scene I.

Suggested Preliminary Practice
Note: If the students have not previously learnt either 'must be' or 'must have (been)', this sketch will probably be too difficult for them, and too much preparation will be required. Assuming, therefore, that the students are familiar with 'must be', here is a suggested practice for 'must have (been)'.

Use a large wall-picture, or draw one, where an accident has taken place, and where it is clear from the positions of the vehicles what happened. For example:

A girl ran across the road. She dropped her doll.
A lorry swerved to avoid it, and hit a tree.
A car braked, and a motor-cyclist crashed into the back of the car.

Point out to the students that, although they did not see these things happen, they can deduce them. Elicit comments such as:

The girl must have run across the road.
The lorry must have swerved.
The car must have braked.

and so on.

Preliminary Questions
1 Name three things that the tourists found in the room.
2 What was the owner of the house doing when they arrived?
3 Why did they give the owner some money?

15

Shakespeare's House

SCENE	The living-room of a house in the town where Shakespeare was born
CHARACTERS	Sidney and Ethel, tourists A man

I *Sidney and Ethel come into the room.*

SIDNEY Well, Ethel, here we are in Shakespeare's front room. This must be where he wrote all his famous tragedies.

ETHEL I'm not surprised, with furniture like this.

SIDNEY What do you mean?

ETHEL Well, look at that armchair. He can't have been comfortable, sitting there.

SIDNEY Don't be silly! He probably sat at this table when he was writing tragedies.

ETHEL Oh, yes . . . Look!

She shows Sidney a typewriter.

This must be Shakespeare's typewriter.

SIDNEY Shakespeare's typewriter?

ETHEL Yes. He must have written all his plays on this.

SIDNEY Ethel! That can't be Shakespeare's typewriter.

ETHEL Why not?

SIDNEY Because Shakespeare didn't *use* a typewriter.

ETHEL Didn't he?

SIDNEY No, of course he didn't. He was a very busy man. He didn't have time to sit in front of a typewriter all day. He probably used a tape-recorder.

ETHEL A tape-recorder?

SIDNEY Yes. I can see him now. He must have sat on this chair, holding his microphone in his hand, saying: 'To be, or not to be.'

ETHEL What does that mean?

SIDNEY Ah well, that is the question.

II ETHEL Sidney, look!

SIDNEY What?

ETHEL Over here. This must be Shakespeare's television.

SIDNEY Shakespeare's television?

ETHEL Yes, it must be. It looks quite old.

SIDNEY Shakespeare didn't have a *television*.

ETHEL Why not?

SIDNEY Why not? Because he went to the theatre every night. He didn't have time to sit at home, watching television.

ETHEL Oh.

They hear someone snoring.

Sidney, what's that? I can hear something. Oh, look!

SIDNEY Where?

ETHEL Over there. There's a man over there, behind the newspaper. I think he's asleep.

SIDNEY Oh, yes. He must be one of Shakespeare's family. He's probably Shakespeare's grandson.

ETHEL Ooh!

SIDNEY I'll just go and say 'Hello'.

He goes over to the man and shouts.

Hello!

MAN What? Eh? What's going on?

III SIDNEY Good morning.

MAN	Good mor – Who are you?
ETHEL	We're tourists.
MAN	Tourists?
SIDNEY	Yes.
ETHEL	It must be very interesting, living here.
MAN	Interesting? Living here? What are you talking about?
SIDNEY	Well, it must be interesting, living in a famous house like this.
MAN	Famous house?
ETHEL	Yes, there must be hundreds of people who want to visit Shakespeare's house.
MAN	Shakespeare's house? Look, there must be some mistake.
SIDNEY	This *is* Shakespeare's house, isn't it?
MAN	*This* is Number 34, Railway Avenue . . . and *I* live here!
ETHEL	Yes. You must be Shakespeare's grandson.
MAN	Shakespeare's grandson?
ETHEL	Yes.
IV SIDNEY	Ethel! Look at this!
ETHEL	What is it?
SIDNEY	Look at it!
	He is holding an ashtray.
ETHEL	Ooh, Shakespeare's ashtray!
SIDNEY	Yes, William Shakespeare's ashtray! Mr Shakespeare, I would like to buy this ashtray as a souvenir of our visit to your grandfather's house.
MAN	For the last time, my name is not –
SIDNEY	I'll give you ten pounds for it.
MAN	Now listen . . . Ten pounds?
SIDNEY	All right then. Twenty pounds.
MAN	Twenty pounds for that ashtray?
ETHEL	Well, it *was* William Shakespeare's ashtray, wasn't it?
MAN	William Shakespeare's . . . Oh, yes, of course. William Shakespeare's ashtray.
	Sidney gives the man twenty pounds.
SIDNEY	Here you are. You're sure twenty pounds is enough . . .
MAN	Well . . .
SIDNEY	All right then. Twenty-five pounds.
	He gives the man another five pounds.
MAN	Thank you. And here's the ashtray.
	The man gives Sidney the ashtray.
SIDNEY	Thank you very much.
ETHEL	I hope we haven't disturbed you too much.
MAN	Not at all. I always enjoy meeting people who know such a lot about Shakespeare. Goodbye.
ETHEL	Goodbye.
	Ethel and Sidney leave.

Listening Comprehension

Questions

I 1 How many tourists were there?
2 Where were they?
3 Why didn't Shakespeare use a typewriter?

II 4 Which tourist knew more about Shakespeare?
5 Were the tourists alone in the room?
6 Describe the man's reaction when he woke up.

III 7 Was the man Shakespeare's grandson?

IV 8 What did the tourists want to take home with them?
9 Why did they want to take it home?
10 Was the man still annoyed when they left?

There are two possible answers to Question 3: one based on the sketch (Sidney's answer), and one the 'real' answer. Question 4 may also provoke some discussion, if Sidney's comments are examined. Make sure that the answer to Question 7 is more than just 'No'; the students should add a comment like 'He can't have been Shakespeare's grandson because . . .'

Reading Comprehension

Impossible!

Read the following 'life history' of Shakespeare and make comments on it.

William Shakespeare was born in Tokyo in 1564 and died in 1697. He wrote his first play at the age of four. He worked as a garage mechanic before becoming a full-time playwright. He didn't leave his home-town until he was twenty-three. In 1584, he bought a car and drove to London. He then travelled widely round Europe, visiting Paris, Berlin, and Rome in the same week. He was a good friend of Charles Dickens and Winston Churchill.

The students should read the text, and then comment on it, using 'can't have (been)' or 'couldn't have (been)'. For example: 'If he was born in 1564, he can't have died in 1697.'* This can be done in groups, with one member of each group noting down the comments. The groups then compare notes.
(* In fact, very little is known about Shakespeare's life except that he was born in Stratford-on-Avon in 1564, married Anne Hathaway, wrote a total of 38 plays and died in 1616.)

Word Puzzle

Do you know where Shakespeare was born? Put the correct words in the vertical columns, and the letters in the box will spell the name of the town.
Read the complete text before you write the words.

The man and the woman in the sketch were (3) . . . . Their names were (1) . . . . and (2) . . . . Shakespeare wrote a lot of (4) . . . . The woman thought that he wrote them on a (8) . . . . The man said that Shakespeare used a tape-recorder, and imagined him with a (7) . . . . in his hand. The man said that Shakespeare was too busy to watch television, because he went to the (5) . . . . every night. They thought the other man was Shakespeare's (9) . . . . They told him he was lucky to live in a (6) . . . . house.

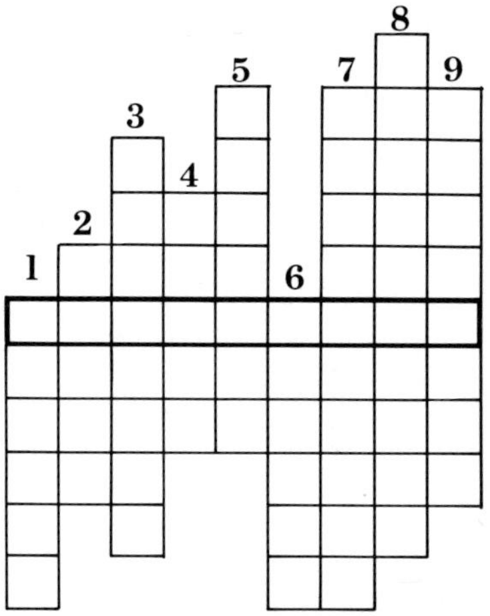

Solution: 1 Sidney 2 Ethel 3 tourists 4 plays 5 theatre 6 famous 7 microphone 8 typewriter 9 grandson. Thus the letters in the box spell 'Stratford'. Stratford-on-Avon is the name of Shakespeare's birthplace.

Communicating

Are You Sure?

A In the sketch, Sidney seems to know a lot about Shakespeare. When someone speaks like this, you may want to make sure they know what they are talking about. These expressions are useful:

> What makes you think so?
> Are you sure?
> How do you know?
> That can't be true.

B When Sidney and Ethel talked about the typewriter, Sidney said 'That can't be Shakespeare's typewriter.' But he did not give the right explanation. You could begin:

> That can't be Shakespeare's typewriter, because . . .

and continue:

> . . . Shakespeare lived 400 years ago.
> . . . typewriters weren't invented then.
> . . . typewriters are modern.

Practise in pairs, talking about the typewriter and the television.

Exercise A: Prompt the students by making some surprising statements for which the evidence is not obvious (e.g. 'Every member of the London Symphony Orchestra is left-handed.'), so that they can react with one of the suggested expressions. They can then practice in pairs, giving their own examples.
Exercise B: The pairs of students can imagine they are in 'Shakespeare's house', like the tourists in the sketch, talking about various objects: the typewriter, the television, and any others they choose (fountain-pen, telephone, record-player, for example). One student makes statements like 'Look – Shakespeare's television!' and the other student makes the sensible comments.

In Your Own Words

Re-enact the sketch in your own words, without reading from the text. Do it in short sections. These words will remind you:

For simple improvised re-enacting in the classroom, this sketch can be done without props although it is useful to have a table and chair to refer to in the first section, and a newspaper (or magazine, or book) for the man to remain behind until he is 'woken up'; an ashtray (or other small object) is also useful, for the fourth section. The students should feel free, as always to include their own ideas, e.g. commenting on other objects in the room.
For a more elaborate 'performance', cameras, sunglasses (not worn throughout, however) and summer clothes are useful for the tourists, and slippers for the man in the house. It is not necessary to have a television on stage. In our version, the television was always indicated by the actors as being in the audience.

Further Role-playing Activities

An Investigation
People often use 'must be' to emphasize that they are sure, even when the facts or evidence are not as clear as they think. Explain this to the students, and then let them try to solve a crime. If they think they know the answer, they should express their idea using 'must be', and other students should challenge them. Here is an example:

A robbery has taken place in an old man's flat in a small block. Draw a diagram on the blackboard, like this:

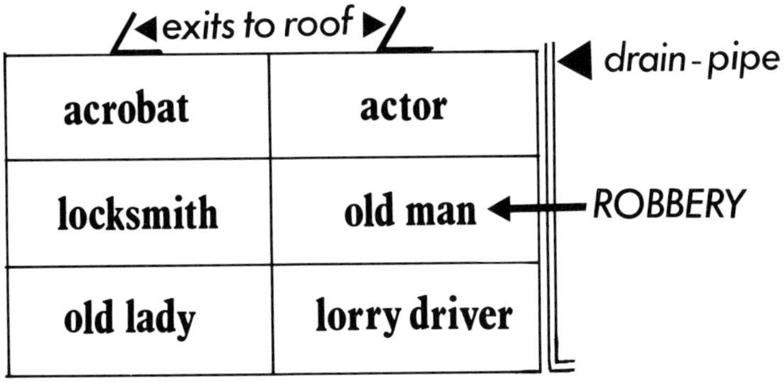

Two students choose roles from the five suspects above, e.g. actor and acrobat. They go out of the classroom and jointly prepare their alibi (where they were, what they were doing at the time of the robbery, etc.). The rest of the class prepare questions and then act as detectives. They ask the two students individually about their alibis. This questioning will probably reveal inconsistencies in the alibis. The class should then give their conclusions, e.g. 'It must have been the actor.' or 'The actor must have done it.' etc.
The activity could be continued by two other students taking different roles.

Pronunciation Practice

'Puzzlement'

In the sketch, the tourists often said things that the man didn't understand. If you are puzzled by what someone says, the natural reaction is to repeat it, as the man did. Point this out to the students, and then re-play the third and fourth sections of the sketch again, stopping at lines such as: 'Interesting? Living here?' and 'Famous house?' so that they can practice the intonation.

Writing

A Dialogue

After the two tourists had left, the man telephoned a friend. This is what the man (A) said. What did his friend (B) say?

A : Hello? Fred, is that you?
B : . . . .
A : I'm fine. You know, something really strange has just happened.
B : . . . .
A : Well, I woke up and found two tourists in my front room.
B : . . . .
A : Because they thought it was *Shakespeare's* house!
B : . . . .
A : No, I'm being serious. They wanted to buy a souvenir of their visit.
B : . . . .
A : Yes, I sold them an ashtray.
B : . . . .
A : Twenty-five pounds.
B : . . . .
A : I'm *not* joking. It's true!

This exercise can be done in groups. Make sure that the students use the 'clues' in deciding what the other speaker in the dialogue said. For example, an answer beginning 'Because . . .' should lead them immediately to a question beginning 'Why . . . ?'; an answer beginning 'Yes, . . .' should lead them to a question without a question-word; an answer with a stressed '*not*' in it should lead them to a previous line which is in direct contradiction. When the dialogues have been completed, the students can read them out as a telephone conversation, adding a conclusion.

What Do You Think?

Souvenirs

When you visit a famous monument or building – a cathedral, for example – you often find shops nearby, selling souvenirs. These are often badly-made, ugly, a horrible colour and very expensive.
Do you think the manufacture of souvenirs like this should be stopped?

In groups, the students can discuss this topic from several angles: Do they buy souvenirs for themselves? For friends or relatives? What kinds of things do they buy? What is their favourite souvenir? Do they think souvenirs are usually expensive? Have they ever argued about the price?
The discussion can be extended to include other 'tourist-traps'. For example, street photographers and ice-cream vendors who ask very high prices. Do the students think there should be laws protecting tourists?

Index

This index lists the language points practised in the sketches and their accompanying exercises.
The numbers refer to pages in this book—the Teachers' Book.
Grammatical points and points of pronunciation (Structure and Usage) are in upright letters.
Attitudes and Functions are *in italics*.
The pages referred to are those containing the introductory outline of the sketch in which the particular point occurs, and also those on which exercises on the particular point can be found (especially exercises in the Communicating, Further Role-playing Activities and Pronunciation Practice sections).